The Story of Peckham and Nunh

by John D. Beasley

London Borough of Southwark
Neighbourhood History No. 3

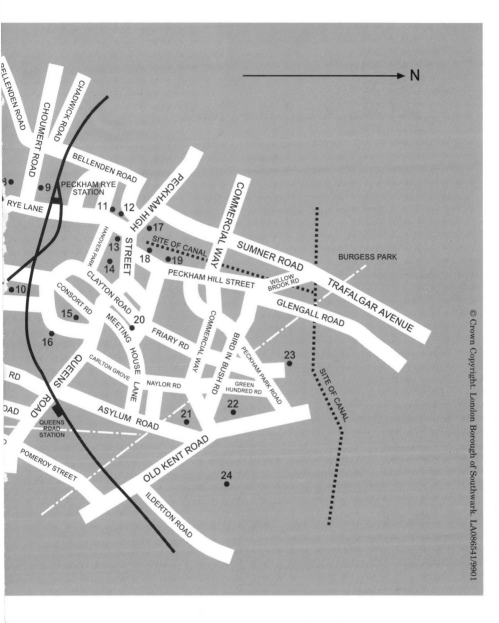

© Crown Copyright. London Borough of Southwark. LA086541/9901

14   Site of Heaton's Folly
15   2 Woods Road
16   Cossall Park
17   Peckham Pulse
18   Peckham Library
19   Site of Peckham Manor House
20   Site of Goldsmith House

21   Caroline Gardens
22   Livesey Museum
23   Site of Windmill
24   Site of South Metropolitan Gas Works

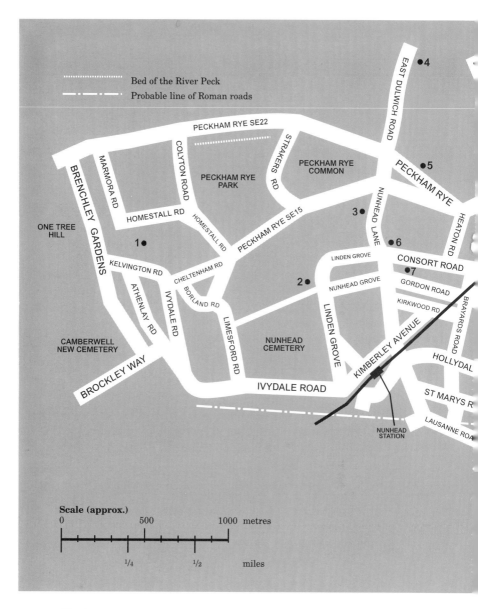

Bed of the River Peck

Probable line of Roman roads

PECKHAM RYE SE22

COLYTON ROAD

PECKHAM RYE PARK

STRAKERS RD

PECKHAM RYE COMMON

EAST DULWICH ROAD

●4

PECKHAM RYE

●5

MARMORA RD

BRENCHLEY GARDENS

HOMESTALL RD

HOMESTALL RD

PECKHAM RYE SE15

NUNHEAD LANE

3●

●6

HEATON RD

ONE TREE HILL

1●

KELVINGTON RD

CHELTENHAM RD

LINDEN GROVE

CONSORT ROAD

●7

ATHENLAY RD

IVYDALE RD

BORLAND RD

2●

NUNHEAD GROVE

GORDON ROAD

KIRKWOOD RD

BRAYARDS ROAD

CAMBERWELL NEW CEMETERY

LIMESFORD RD

NUNHEAD CEMETERY

LINDEN GROVE

KIMBERLEY AVENUE

HOLLYDAL

BROCKLEY WAY

IVYDALE ROAD

ST MARYS R

NUNHEAD STATION

LAUSANNE ROA

Scale (approx.)

0   500   1000   metres

1/4   1/2   miles

Key to map

1	Honor Oak Reservoir and Aquarius Golf Club	7	Nunhead Library
2	Nunhead Reservoirs	8	Sri Chinmoy Peace Garden
3	Former Steam Bus Garage	9	Former Palyn's Alms-Houses
4	London Wildlife Garden Centre	10	Site of Nazareth House
5	Troy Town	11	Former Quaker Meeting House
6	Beeston's Alms-Houses	12	Site of Basing Manor House
		13	The Aylesham Centre

First published 1976 and revised in 1983

This new edition 1999
© London Borough of Southwark

Southwark Local Studies Library
211 Borough High Street
LONDON SE1 IJA

ISBN 0 905849 26 4
British Library Cataloguing in Publication data
A catalogue record for this book is available from the British Library

Front cover:
Watercolour of Peckham Rye by J.B. Cuming showing the River Peck
and the White Horse inn in the background, 1828.
Inside front cover
Nunhead Hill from fields on the Peckham side.
A 19th century watercolour by J.A. Poulter.
Inside back cover
A postcard of the southern end of Rye Lane looking north, c1905.

London Borough of Southwark Neighbourhood Histories

Contents

Preface and acknowledgements

"Is there life in Peckham?" asked comedian Alexei Sayle.
Undoubtedly there is! Readers of this book may be surprised by
Peckham's long and interesting past. Although I have written
eight other books on Peckham and Nunhead, it has been an
enjoyable experience to cover many aspects of the area's history
which have not been included in previous publications.

Various people have provided valuable assistance and I am
particularly grateful to Len Reilly, Stephen Humphrey and
Steve Potter, who run the excellent Southwark Local Studies
Library. Their plentiful knowledge and enthusiasm are readily
shared with all visitors to the library. Gill Frost made numerous
helpful suggestions and useful information was provided by
Philip W. Bradley, Pam Elven, Tony Fletcher, Harvey Sheldon,
Ron Woollacott and The Showmen's Guild of Great Britain.
Thanks are also due to Charles Phillips for helping the text
to shine even brighter and to Carol Enright for designing
the layout and seeing the book through the printing process.

Acknowledgement is also given to the South London Gallery for
permission to reproduce the pictures on the front cover, the inside
front cover and on p.27. Thanks are also due to the London
Transport Museum for permission to reproduce the picture on
p.35; to the Pictorial Press for the image on p.66; and to Peter
Mackertich and Southwark Building Design Service for the
picture on p.92.

People's lives are enriched by local history. The more they know
about their locality, the more interesting the area becomes to
them – it is knowledge that makes dull streets spring to life.
As I travel around SE15 and the surrounding area I am conscious
of the fascinating history that people can enjoy in the southern
part of the London Borough of Southwark.

In Peckham and Nunhead exciting changes are taking place,
so it was easy and a real pleasure to write a positive final chapter
outlining how SE15 is improving. Among the area's many

post-war housing developments is William Margrie Close, named after the self-styled "Sage of Peckham" who founded the London Explorers' Club. His writings contain the line: "I have no very urgent desire to go to Heaven; Peckham is good enough for me." As the area continues to become a more pleasant place in which to live, a growing number of residents may wish to echo his views.

John D. Beasley
Peckham 1999

Introduction

The popular TV comedy series *Only Fools and Horses* made Peckham's name well-known throughout Britain in the 1990s but it did not present an accurate image of this fascinating part of South London. Life in Peckham stretches back far beyond written history. Evidence has been found that people lived in the area about 6,000 years ago.

The name Peckham is much more recent and stems from the Old English *Peac-ham* meaning "village by a hill". The hill may have been the one at Honor Oak, but manorial and other evidence strongly suggests that it was Nunhead Hill which is now in Nunhead Cemetery.

The origin of the name Nunhead is shrouded in mystery. It was mentioned in a deed dated March 1583 in which Edgar Scot sold to Thomas and William Patching a fifth part of the manor of Camberwell Buckingham, including certain estates "lying at Nunn-head". There is no evidence to link the name Nunhead with the famed "Nun of Kent", Elizabeth Barton (?1506–34), whose outspoken criticism of Henry VIII's marriage with Anne Boleyn led to her being executed for treason at Tyburn. However, the name may be connected to the nunnery of St John the Baptist at Halliwell (Shoreditch), which acquired various lands in Camberwell and Peckham in the late 12th century. These later formed the manor of Camberwell Friern. The name None Head is shown on John Rocque's map of the area dated 1741-45.

Peckham and Nunhead, like many places in London, used to be hamlets and were absorbed into the metropolis only during the 19th century. Administratively they were part of the County of Surrey before the London County Council was formed in 1889. When the metropolitan boroughs were established in 1900, as a separate tier of local government functioning alongside the LCC, Peckham and Nunhead became part of the Metropolitan Borough of Camberwell. In 1965 they joined the London Borough of Southwark, which was created from the former Metropolitan Boroughs of Bermondsey, Camberwell and Southwark.

Numbered postal districts were introduced as a wartime measure in 1917 to assist inexperienced women workers with the task of sorting mail. Peckham and Nunhead are usually thought to be covered by SE15, but in fact the areas spread into other postal districts. This book covers the history of the whole of SE15 and of small parts bordering it in SE1, SE5, SE22 and SE23.

The Peckham Society, founded in 1975 as the amenity society for SE15, has pointed out that there are more books currently available on Peckham and Nunhead than on any other part of Southwark. The best general studies of the area are *Ye Parish of Camerwell* by W.H. Blanch, published in 1875, and H.J. Dyos' *Victorian Suburb,* published in 1961. In addition, there are many books on particular aspects – including architecture, churches, name origins, people and transport – and on particular locations, including Nunhead Cemetery and Peckham Rye Park. See the Booklist for further details.

The growing number of books on this formerly neglected area of London contain a treasure trove of information. Among the precious nuggets are the following:

John Reagan, whose grandson became President of the USA, was born where the Friary Estate is today; Norma Major, wife of former Prime Minister John Major, was a pupil at Peckham School. The first British-born Conservative woman MP, Mabel Philipson, was born where the Copeland Road car park now stands. Will Thorne, MP for West Ham, worked in the Old Kent Road gasworks and Lord Murray, who was General Secretary of the Trades Union Congress, lived in Talfourd Road.

On Peckham Rye William Blake had the first of many mystical visions; Charles Dickens had a secret love affair in Linden Grove; Robert Browning received his early education in the High Street; James Murray, the first editor of the Oxford English Dictionary, lived in Nunhead and Denman Road; Edgar Wallace, the writer whose idea was made into the 1933 film *King Kong*, attended Reddins Road School.

H.J. Heinz's first factory in England was in Peckham; Ilford Limited was started by Alfred Harman who ran a photographic shop in the High Street before moving to Ilford; London's last cowkeeper, John Jorden, ran a dairy in Lugard Road. Another firm which began as a dairy, Austin's, became one of Europe's largest second-hand and antique dealers; the last firm in the world to make wooden hand-made cameras, Gandolfi, was based in Nunhead.

John Wesley, founder of Methodism, wrote his final will while staying in Peckham; Dr Alfred Salter and his wife Ada attended the Quaker Meeting House in what is now Highshore Road. Dame Elizabeth Cadbury, who did much social work and was married to the chocolate manufacturer George Cadbury, was born at Peckham Rye; Dr Harold Moody, who founded the League of Coloured Peoples, lived in Peckham – and his former house bears Peckham's only blue plaque. Percy Lane Oliver, founder of the blood donor service, carried out much of his early work in a house overlooking Peckham Rye Park.

Former England cricketer John Emburey was born in Meeting House Lane; golfer Sir Henry Cotton attended Ivydale Road School; the young Tommy Steele practised playing his guitar in rooms in Rye Lane later used as business premises by Russian spy Gordon Lonsdale; songwriter Tommie Connor was inspired to write "The Biggest Aspidistra in the world" by an aspidistra in Evelina Road; and a doctor who lived in Queen's Road during the 19th century was the proud owner of Oliver Cromwell's skull!

Peckham and Nunhead have been home and workplace to a wide range of people, famous and less famous. Countless residents have made positive contributions to the local community and to the wider world. In his foreword to the book *Who Was Who in Peckham* the Rt Rev David Sheppard, who lived in Asylum Road when he was Bishop of Woolwich and was made a Life Peer in 1998, wrote: "In its changing life Peckham has continued to have a mixed community. That multi-cultural and multi-racial community has marvellous potential for harmonious and creative living."

6,000 years of history

During the redevelopment of the site where the Cantium Retail
Park now stands in the Old Kent Road, many important
archaeological finds were made. Today shoppers can visit Halfords
and B&Q, then go to McDonald's and learn from a photographic
display that the oldest finds date from the Mesolithic period (the
Middle Stone Age, 6,000 years ago) and the Neolithic period (New
Stone Age, 5,000 years ago). At that time the site was a production
centre for flint tools. More than 1,780 flints were found there,
including arrowheads, blades and scrapers.

In another part of Peckham, a 5,000-year-old polished flint axehead
was dug up in the back garden of 2 Martock Court, Consort Road,
in 1967; it is stored in the Cuming Museum, Walworth Road.
According to experts at the British Museum, it is the only
axehead of its kind to have been found in this part of the country.
It was embedded in white clay at a depth of two feet.

After the Neolithic period there seems to have been a long
interval before activity recommenced on the site of the Cantium
Retail Park. Excavators found Roman pottery there and also
gravel surfaces, which may have been part of a roadway. Roman
Watling Street undoubtedly ran close to where the Old Kent Road
is today. This highway ran from Richborough in Kent to Chester
via London and St Albans, and formed an important part of the
Romano-British transport system.

Archaeologist Harvey Sheldon has suggested that Queen's Road
and Peckham High Street may be on the line of another Roman
road south of Watling Street, connecting an up-river crossing of
the Thames (in the Vauxhall area) with Watling Street at New
Cross. No proof has been found but a Roman urn was dug up in
the High Street in the 18th century.

A little more than a thousand years after the Romans invaded
England, the Domesday Book (1085-6) was compiled. That
recorded a settlement at "Pecheham", held by the Bishop of
Lisieux, which comprised two hides (about 240 acres), land for
one plough, one villager (a peasant farmer) and three
smallholders (who each held a few acres) and two acres of

meadow. Pecheham was valued at 30 shillings. It was clearly a small place in the 11th century.

By the time the Domesday Book was compiled, the manorial system was established throughout most of England. A manor was an estate held by a landlord who was himself a tenant of the Crown or of a lord who held land directly from the Crown. A manor was an economic and administrative unit. The lord of the manor retained part of the land for his own use, while tenants farmed the remainder – apart from the land that was kept uncultivated on a rotation basis so it could be replenished.

Although records for the medieval period are scarce, it is thought that in 1300 there was probably a hamlet near Nunhead called Bredinghurst. The Bretinghurst family lived at the manor house of Bretinghurst or Bredinghurst and were involved in local affairs for over 100 years. Sir Reynolde de Bretinghurst was a local knight. Knights were obliged to perform military service in exchange for the lands granted to them.

The Bretinghurst manor was a widely dispersed estate with lands both north and south of Peckham village. This suggests that although by the 17th century the manor house was near Peckham High Street, it had earlier been at Nunhead. A house called Bridinghurst and a lane called Bridinghurst Hills were near Nunhead according to a 17th century deed.

In the 14th century another hamlet near the south end of where Rye Lane is today had the Anglo-Saxon settlement name Worth. A large arable field lay between Peckham and Nunhead. The earliest names for it date from the 16th century when different parts were known as Bursted, Brayard and the Brade. Brayards Road is a reminder of this field.

In the 14th century Peckham and Basing manors existed. Peckham Manor House was on the west side of where Peckham Hill Street is today; the new library will occupy what is thought to be part of the grounds. Basing Manor House stood close to where Peckham High Street and Bellenden Road intersect today.

Dovedale manor had 144 acres in 1298; the manor house may have been near where the junction of Southampton Way and Peckham Grove is today. Bredinghurst had 144 acres in 1336.

In the tax rolls for all the Surrey villages in the 13th century, Peckham and Camberwell were listed together and had 55 people over the tax threshold, suggesting that these villages were fairly prosperous. Farming was the principal economic activity.

1500-1750: Surrey hamlets grow

Between the early 16th century and 1750 Peckham and Nunhead gradually grew from Surrey hamlets into villages. The land was fertile and the mild climate favourable for agriculture – most of the inhabitants earned their living from the land.

The population was small. In the parish of Camberwell, which included Peckham and Nunhead, the average number of annual births between 1580 and 1589 was 23 (with 26 deaths). The equivalent figures for 1680-1689 were 38 and 52. The population of Camberwell parish in 1787 was 3,762. There were about 770 houses.

Then, as at other times, rich and poor people lived in Peckham. After John Wesley, the founder of Methodism, had delivered a sermon in the open air in Peckham on 8 January 1789 he wrote in his Journal: "Here in the evening, I preached to a very serious congregation, although many of them were of the better rank. But rich and poor seemed equally determined to work out their salvation."

St Giles' in Camberwell was the parish church covering Peckham and attendance at Sunday services was compulsory until 1650. The affairs of the parish were run by the Vestry, a committee of prominent men who met in the vestry room of the Church and raised rates, or local taxes, to pay for the services they provided. In 1651 the Rev John Maynard, who had resigned as Vicar of Camberwell after declaring himself a Puritan, went to live in a road known today as Meeting House Lane. He first preached in his own house and then in 1657 a meeting house was built. From there the congregation moved to a new chapel in Rye Lane in 1717.

A survivor of the late 17th century stands at 2 Woods Road, where what may be Peckham's oldest building is home to a scaffolding firm. This building – called Gloster House on some old maps – has undergone many changes over the years.

At the other end of Peckham High Street, Melon Road is a reminder that Sir Thomas Gardyner, who lived at Basing Manor House, sent some melons to King Charles I after the King had

Basing Manor House, seen from the south, in a painting by
C. Dewley of 1872.

visited him and given him "a fat venison in melon time". Sir
Thomas was Lord of the Manor and one of the Justices of the
Peace for Surrey.

In the following century naturalist Peter Collinson (1694-1768)
carried out experiments with exotic plants in the garden of his
Peckham house. He found it a peaceful setting and in 1731 he
wrote: "I have here retreated from the hurrys of the town and
breathe the air of content and quiet, being the centre of my
humble wishes, a little cottage, a pretty garden, well filled, a
faithful loving partner, a little prattling boye, the pledge of mutual
love, surrounded with these blessings I pronounce myself happy."

Collinson was visited in 1748 by Peter Kalm, a Swedish traveller
who was en route to America. Kalm wrote: "June 10, in the
afternoon, I went to Peckham, a pretty village which lies 3 miles
from London in Surrey, where Mr Peter Collinson has a beautiful
little garden, full of all kinds of the rarest plants, especially
American ones, which can endure the English climate and stand
out the whole winter. However neat and small it is there is
scarcely a garden where so many kinds of trees and plants,
especially the rarest, are to be found."

1750-1900: The early modern period

Villages become part of London

John Rocque's map (1741–5) shows Peckham and Nunhead covered with fields. In 1750 Peckham was a small Surrey village with most houses clustered around the High Street.

Peckham Lane, now Queen's Road, ran east towards New Cross. Another road led west to Camberwell. Old Meeting House Lane led to Kent Street, now Old Kent Road. A road, now Peckham Park Road, bisected the 240-acre North Field, and led to Peckham Gap at its junction with Kent Street. Another road, now Trafalgar Avenue, cut through fields to Kent Street.

South Street, now Rye Lane, led to Peckham Rye where the northern part of the common was surrounded by a few houses. The common was bisected by roads leading from Goose Green to None Head, now Nunhead, which had a few houses on the northern and western sides of what today is Nunhead Green.

Peckham Manor House was owned by Mrs Martha Hill, after whom Peckham Hill Street was named. She bought it in 1732 after the previous owner, Lord Trevor, died there in 1730. Lord Trevor was Lord Chief Justice from 1701 until 1714.

Dr John Milner ran a boarding school where in about 1756 Oliver Goldsmith – later author of the dramatic comedy *She Stoops to Conquer* – worked as an usher. It stood at the corner of what are now Goldsmith Road and Staffordshire Street; today a plaque commemorates the playwright's educational work in Peckham.

The area developed slowly over the next 80 years. By the time Dewhirst produced his map of the parish of Camberwell in 1842, Peckham village had more houses and other buildings; there was still a hamlet centred around Nun Green. The High Street was lined with houses. Among them were the Kentish Drovers, Red Bull and Red Cow public houses, so named to attract the trade of cattle drovers from country to the south and east who used Peckham as a last staging and grazing point before moving on to London markets.

PARISH OF S.ᵗ PAUL DEPTFORD

New roads had been built to the west of Rye Lane. Elm Grove, South Grove (now Holly Grove), Blenheim Grove, Choumert Place (now Road) all had houses in them. South Grove included a shrubbery which was bigger than Holly Grove Shrubbery is today. Residents contributed up to thirty shillings a year to keep the road, footpath and shrubbery in repair. Trustees were chosen by the tenants annually under an 1831 deed of George Choumert, after whom Choumert Road was named.

Marlborough House stood in its own grounds north of the High Street, where Marmont Road is today. It was an old mansion believed to have been a residence for members of the Marlborough family. The mansion contained a noble entrance hall and had a fine oak staircase. Frescoes adorned the walls and ceilings. Opposite Marlborough House, on the south side of the High Street, stood Blenheim House which is thought to have been a minor building belonging to the mansion.

In the High Street stood Peckham House, where Warwick Park School is today. This fine old mansion was the home of the wealthy Spitta family who lived there in great style and gave fetes. They were generous to the poor who lived nearby. The building became a private lunatic asylum in 1826. In the 1870s the asylum had 350 inmates drawn from all classes of society "from the pauper inmate to the titled dame", as W.H. Blanch wrote in *Ye Parish of Camerwell*.

Pelican House School was established in about 1825 where Kingfisher House in Peckham Road is today. The building it occupied had been erected before 1675. The stone pelicans, from which the name was derived, originally stood on brick pilasters at the entrance gates.

Heaton's Folly stood in the centre of Peckham village, where the Safeway car park is today. It was built before 1792 by philanthropist Isaac Heaton who lived in a large brick mansion

Opposite: Peckham and Nunhead as shown in the Dewhirst map of the parish of Camberwell in 1842.

Heaton's Folly, 1810.

with a very extensive lawn to the south. Near the southern
extremity stood an ornamental building, consisting of a lofty
square tower, which was a very conspicuous object in the local
countryside. Mr Heaton had the folly built by about 500 men
during a very severe winter in order to provide them with work.

North of the High Street most of the land was used for market
gardens and growing crops. Houses lined the Old Kent Road and
some houses existed in Peckham New Town, the area
surrounding what today is Peckham Park Road. The New Town
was the first local example of planned development and was
promoted by the Hill family who owned the land. The Rosemary
Branch public house stood at the corner of what today are
Commercial Way and Southampton Way.

Gasworks, which started producing coal gas in 1833, were at the
side of the Grand Surrey Canal, north of the Old Kent Road.
Another public house called the Kentish Drovers was nearby and
still exists at the corner of Commercial Way.

Bryant's 1823 map shows a windmill – which was used to grind corn – a few yards to the south-east of St George's Church, at the corner of what today are St George's Way and Wells Way. Another mill stood close to the Old Kent Road, west of where Livesey Place is today.

The Licensed Victuallers' Asylum in Asylum Road, off the Old Kent Road, housed retired publicans. Unlike this asylum, which was in a built-up area, Beeston's Gift Almshouses, which had been built in 1834 in what today is Consort Road, were surrounded by fields.

Development south of the High Street towards Nunhead was more patchy than between Peckham village and the Old Kent Road. Apart from market gardens, there was a brick field. The White Horse public house stood where the present pub with that name stands at Peckham Rye.

Only a handful of houses surrounded Nun Green, now Nunhead Green. Further south was Homestall Farm where Peckham Rye Park is today. Large houses occupied by wealthy people lined both sides of Peckham Rye and there was a tile kiln. The River Peck ran across the common; there was also a lake, a few yards north of where the lido was later built.

When Nunhead was a small hamlet surrounded by market gardens and open fields, Nunhead Hill was chosen as the site for a new cemetery. As the population grew in the first half of the 19th century, the churchyards became overcrowded and insanitary. The London Cemetery Company, which had opened its first cemetery at Highgate, decided to create All Saints' Cemetery at Nunhead. This was done under "An Act for establishing cemeteries for the Interment of the Dead, Northward, Southward, and Eastward of the Metropolis, by a Company to be called the London Cemetery Company", dated 17 August 1836.

The new 52-acre cemetery was consecrated on 29 July 1840 by the Bishop of Winchester, Charles Richard Sumner; Nunhead was then in the Winchester diocese. Sumner Road was named after

the Bishop. The previous year, when the cemetery was laid
out, two lodges were built as residence and offices for the
superintendent who was to look after the day-to-day functioning
of the cemetery. They were designed by James Bunstone
Bunning, the architect who designed the cemetery's layout.

Two temporary chapels were also built. These were replaced
by permanent ones in 1844. The arson-damaged Anglican
chapel still exists but the Dissenters' chapel was destroyed
when it was bombed during World War II. The Anglican chapel
included a carriage porch and a crypt, which is now sealed.
The paved floor of the chapel contained an eight-foot by four-foot
opening through which coffins were lowered to the vaults below.
Anyone could be buried in the cemetery but not everyone could
afford the fees so it was used mainly for gentlemen and
tradesmen and their families.

Henry Daniel was the first monumental mason to establish a
yard at Nunhead. His workshops were opposite the cemetery's
main gates. His business flourished and he built a large Gothic
house next to his workshops. He lived there with his family until
he died in 1867, aged 62, and was buried in his family vault in
Nunhead Cemetery. After the cemetery closed in 1969 Henry
Daniel's old house and workshop were demolished.

Preston and Company were local masons whose premises in
Gibbon Road, close to the cemetery, were established before
1855. David Cripps Preston ran the firm for many years and was
a proprietor of the London Cemetery Company. He was a
Baptist and erected many of the memorials in the dissenters'
part of the cemetery.

In the 30 years after the cemetery had been opened, Peckham
saw further developments. By the 1870s dozens of streets had
been built on arable land. The first large scale Ordnance Survey
Map (1870) shows how the outward movement of population from
the city had had a noticeable effect on Peckham. The area was
now a segment of a swelling city, whose population grew from
about 865,000 in 1801 to over 4.5 million in 1901. The population

in the Peckham Registration Sub-District increased from 12,563 in 1841 to 93,033 in 1901; the most rapid periods of growth were 1841–51 and 1871–81.

During the 19th century there was a movement of population out of the crowded centre of London to the suburbs, where the air was fresher and the water was clean. In *The Wilds of London*, published in 1874, James Greenwood quoted an inhabitant of a central London slum who referred with envy to "Peckham and them airy parts". In the second half of the century the activities of entrepreneurial developers and the increase in affordable transport speeded up suburban growth. Newcomers to Peckham included people from various parts of Britain, Ireland and abroad.

By now little spare land existed in the heart of Peckham. Not only had many houses been built, but so had two breweries - Peckham Brewery in Hill Street and Hope Brewery in the High Street, between Stafford Street and the police station. A dye works was next to Gloster House, now 2 Woods Road, and a laundry had been built in Meeting House Lane. A fire station was opened in Peckham Road in 1867. The building still exists next to the present fire station. A new police station was opened in the High Street in 1893.

By the 1870s North Peckham, which had begun life as a middle-class suburb of the New Town but then became a poorer area, was crowded with houses and other buildings – including churches and schools. Work for local people was found in the South Metropolitan Gas Works and in the timber yards on the banks of the Grand Surrey Canal, which also provided work for boatmen. There were also a laundry and basket manufactory south of the Old Kent Road, as well as Britannia Brewery, Whiting Works, Glengall Works (Patent Safe Manufactory) and Glengall Cabinet Manufactory. Cottage Farm still existed next to Ossory Road and the canal. North of the Old Kent Road was another brewery, a floor cloth manufactory and Japan Works. Japanning was a process in which various materials were lacquered, most often in black, to provide them with a durable and sometimes decorative finish.

South of the High Street, roads had been developed surrounding
Rye Lane but there were plenty of fields to the east and south.
Surrounding St Mary Magdalen School and stretching to Beeston's
Gift Almshouses in Albert (now Consort) Road were more fields.

Peckham Rye was surrounded by large houses with long
gardens but there were fields between the houses on the east
side of the Rye and Linden Grove. Adjoining Peckham Rye
was Homestall Farm. A few houses existed in Sartor Road
and Newlands.

Builders move in

Builders changed the face of the area in the 19th century. In 1808
the de Crespigny family, Huguenot refugees from France who had
settled in Camberwell at the end of the 17th century, bought a
number of scattered pieces of land lying to the east of Rye Lane.
These were let mainly for agricultural purposes before the 1830s.
One area they owned included Heaton's Folly and the surrounding
grounds on the east side of Rye Lane; another was an area
between Rye Lane and the Nunhead footpath from Queen's Road.
The de Crespigny family bought the latter estate in 1841.

In about 1870 numerous builders, mostly local men, began to
develop the whole of the land bounded by the railway, Rye Lane,
Hanover Park and Clayton Road. Most of the new roads –
Clayton, McKerrell, Cerise and Raul Roads, Moncrieff Street and
Hanover Park – were laid and populated during the 1870s, when
about 150 houses went up, but the process was not completed
before the end of the 1880s.

The other de Crespigny estate further along Rye Lane was built
up between 1864 and 1886. The demand for workers' housing in
the area was high. The introduction of cheaper workmen's fares
on the railway in the 1880s made it possible for working-class
people to live in the Peckham area and work in central London.
The period also saw the relocation of a number of industries from
central London to the suburbs.

*The Old Rosemary Branch public house in Southampton Way,
a view of 1775.*

Between Peckham Grove and Cator Street there was a gradual
disposal of a large estate which, at the end of the 18th century,
had been in the hands of the Shard family. By 1834 the land had
come into the possession of Charrington, the London coal
merchant, who sold it to Richard Nicholl of Barnet. He died in
1838 and left it to his family. Grosvenor Road and Peckham
Grove, which gave access to the area, were cut and building
began. Maps suggest that a grid pattern of streets had been
conceived for the development of the whole area lying between
Peckham Grove and Sumner Road.

Though most of this larger area was developed in this way, the
19 acres that lay between Peckham Grove and Cator Street had a
different treatment. This area was sold to James Smith, landlord
of the Rosemary Branch tavern, which stood where the junction
of Southampton Way and Commercial Way is today. In 1864
Smith sold about seven acres of it to form a small building estate
consisting of Blake's Road and Hornby Road, which was built up

19

in the next 15 years. The remaining land was kept for some years
as a cricket field and a place of amusement attached to the
tavern, but it too was auctioned in 1867. It then changed hands
at a rapidly advancing price at least three times in the next five
years, before being bought in 1875 by local magistrate Richard
Strong. The new owner arranged for five new roads with about
240 houses to be built.

Lyndhurst Road (now Way) was developed in the 1840s. Talfourd
Road and Denman Road were carved out by the British Land
Company in 1857–62. Between 1842 and 1846 a terrace of seven
brick and stucco villas was built by Benjamin Southall on the
west side of the footpath to Peckham, which ran southwards from
the Lord Nelson public house in Old Kent Road. This is now
2-14 Trafalgar Avenue and includes The Trafalgar Surgery at
number 10. To the south, the British Land Company developed
the 40-acre Peckham Rye estate, between Camberwell Grove
and Bellenden Road between 1872 and 1874.

Occasionally a company disposed of the freehold of an estate
without having made any preparations for building development.
A quarter of the Peckham Rye estate was left undeveloped in this
way between 1872 and 1875. It was then sold in one lot as the
Denmark Place estate and the familiar process of development on
building lease was carried on by a score of different builders over
the following four or five years. This process worked as follows:
the freeholder would grant a developer a building lease, typically
of 99 years, and sometimes specified the type of house to be built.
The builder would profit by renting the houses he had erected but
at the end of the lease the houses would become the property of
the freeholder.

In the north Peckham Park was developing so quickly in the
1870s that *The Builder* stated in 1876 that it was "fast losing its
suburban character ... and promises shortly to form a little town
in itself". This area was the Duke of Marlborough's former estate
between the High Street and the Old Kent Road, bounded on the
north-east by Asylum Road and on the north-west by Commercial
Road (now Way). This development had been going on since about

1850, when Marlborough House and a 1,000-yard extension of
Marlborough Road were auctioned.

In Nunhead, between the 1880s and 1907 Edward Yates, one of
the largest builders in South London, had built 742 houses on the
Waverley Park Estate. It was his largest building project and one
of the biggest enterprises of any builder in South London. The
estate originally consisted of four fields of about 19 acres on the
east and south sides of Nunhead Cemetery. Yates bought the
freehold of this land in 1877 from T.W. Evans MP; he began by
turning part of the land into a brickfield and by the summer of
1878 was interesting local builders in his bricks.

What may have decided Yates to develop the estate himself was
the opportunity to lease from Christ's Hospital two pieces of land
adjoining his own freehold land to the south. In 1881 or 1882 he
also bought an estate of about 17 acres adjoining the Christ's
Hospital estate on its southern side. Next he bought another
piece of ground of about six acres known as "The Vista". By the
end of 1884 Yates had formed out of four separate parts a
reasonably compact and accessible estate of about 50 acres. He
began in January of that year to erect the first houses in Ivydale
Road, the backbone of the estate. Of the 2,345 houses which Yates
owned in 1905, practically at the end of his business career,
nearly one-third were located at Nunhead.

Two building societies were set up in the 19th century so that
people could borrow money to buy their own homes. The Peckham
Permanent Benefit Building Society was formed in 1855. This
amalgamated with the Paddington Building Society in 1981. The
Peckham Mutual Permanent Building Society started in 1879.
This became known as the Peckham Building Society and was
amalgamated with the Cheltenham and Gloucester Building
Society in 1990.

As the population grew, an increasing number of men were
employed in building houses, roads, sewers, shops, factories,
schools and churches. Work was available for bricklayers, joiners,
painters, plumbers and labourers.

New jobs

In 1750 most residents in Peckham and Nunhead were involved in agriculture, but the 19th century witnessed major changes in occupations. Countless new jobs were created as Peckham and Nunhead ceased to be villages and became an integral part of an expanding metropolis.

After the Grand Surrey Canal from Greenland Dock to Camberwell was completed in 1811, it was decided to cut a branch to Peckham. Digging this extension in 1825–6 provided work for many men. When it was completed, new jobs were created: saw mills sprang up on its banks and the waterway was used for transporting market garden produce and bulky goods such as road metal, coal, and particularly timber and other building materials.

As transport systems developed, more jobs were created running omnibuses and horse-drawn trams. When the railway system was extended to Peckham and Nunhead in the 1860s, many men were involved in building tracks and stations. The expansion of the railways – and especially the introduction of cheap workmen's fares in the 1880s – enabled many people to live in Peckham and Nunhead and work further afield. This created a demand for housing that was the impetus behind many of the area's large developments.

The gas industry was another source of employment. The first distributor of gas in Peckham was the Phoenix Gas Light & Coke Company, which had consumers in Peckham New Town by 1831. The South Metropolitan Gas Company was its rival. By the end of 1834 over 20 miles of mains radiated from South Metropolitan's works by the Grand Surrey Canal near the Old Kent Road.

The growth in shops also stimulated jobs. By the end of the 1860s, Rye Lane already had a number of well-established shops. Its development as a shopping centre was given a major boost by the expansion of Jones and Higgins' departmental store, which began as a drapery shop in 1867 at 3 Rye Lane. In about 1882 Henry Holdron's "Market" – another important business – opened at 53 Rye Lane. Many shops were opened not just in Rye Lane and the

Jones and Higgins' store. A view from The Warehouseman and Draper
of 2 May 1896.

High Street but also in back streets. Corner shops, with living
accommodation at the rear and upstairs, were a common sight.

At Nunhead, work was available in a firework factory run by
Charles Thomas Brock. In 1870, at the time of the Franco-
Prussian war, Brock was asked to manufacture two million
cartridge tubes for the French War Department.

Many young women became servants in the 19th century.
Other jobs were created in factories, dairies and public houses
when Peckham changed from a rural to a suburban community.
Jobs were available in Peckham Flour Mill in Clayton Road,
the Tramway Depot in Basing Road (now Bellenden Road),
a smithy in Hill Street, a brewery in Chadwick Road (where Print
Village is today), the British Wine Manufactory in Russell Road,
a pottery and laundry in Gordon Road, Bussey's sports goods
factory to the east of Peckham Rye Station (where it can still be
seen), and in a laundry and enamel works between Caulfield
Road and Stanbury Road.

Help for poor people

Some Peckham residents who had inherited money and property from wealthy ancestors lived in grand houses, employed servants and had their own coaches. Others, in sharp contrast, were poor. When William Hone, writer and bookseller, lived at Rose Cottage close to Peckham Rye, he usually kept the pump on his well fastened to prevent tramps from making too free a use of it.

As a result of the Poor Law Amendment Act 1834, a Board of Guardians of the Poor was appointed in the parish of Camberwell in 1835. The Board took over the work of caring for poor people from the members of the parish Vestry, who had made payments to destitute and despairing residents from money raised by a rate or tax on property owners. The new Board's first annual report shows that on 31 December 1835 the total number of indoor poor (i.e. those living in the parish workhouse) was 267 – 75 men, 126 women and 66 children. In the same year 1,700 people received outdoor relief (i.e. assistance to prevent the necessity to be admitted to a workhouse) - 242 men, 538 women and 920 children.

The new Board had a rigorous approach, fully demonstrated by the fact that the following year the number receiving outdoor relief was cut to 605. This sharp fall did not come about because there were fewer poor people but because the Board simply refused payment to many people claiming relief. The report stated: "The board have in their possession a list of no less than 207 persons, the greater portion of whom are still resident within the parish ... who under the old system were regular in their attendance at the board for parochial relief, but are now maintaining themselves and their families solely by their own industry and labour ... in the former case, while they leaned on parochial aid, most of them bore idle and dissolute characters, their families were ragged and starved, and their hovels filthy and wretched. In the latter case, now that they depend on their own energies, they readily find employment – are reported industrious; whilst their children are decently clad and go to school, and their dwellings present the appearance which would be desired in the cottage of an English labourer."

In 1846 the number of people who received relief was 1,429. Four years later this grew to 4,584. A workhouse was provided in Peckham in 1867 after nuns moved out of Nazareth House, in what today is Gordon Road, due to the railway destroying the privacy of the grounds. In 1873 *The Metropolitan* reported that 110 aged and infirm male paupers lived in Nazareth House. The inmates, many of whom had been tradesmen in the parish, engaged in various industrial pursuits. The four acres of grounds were used for keeping pigs and poultry as well as for growing potatoes, parsnips, onions, carrots, rhubarb, lettuces and other produce. The inmates made a pony cart and Venetian blinds. Others worked as blacksmiths.

Peckham's swelling population meant that the number of paupers in the area increased, and so another workhouse was needed. A new one was built in the grounds of Nazareth House and opened in 1879. Each inmate at the workhouse, which became known as The Spike, had to earn a night's lodging by breaking a certain amount of stone into pieces small enough to go through a grille; one is preserved at the Livesey Museum, Old Kent Road.

The Spike remained as a Camberwell Poor Law Union workhouse until 1930, when the Boards of Guardians who ran Poor Law Unions were abolished under the Local Government Act 1929 and the workhouse became a common lodging house. The huge building was converted into flats in the early 1990s. Cross Close was built on the site of Nazareth House; a large cross was at the top of the building – hence the name of the Close.

Peckham had two other workhouses during the 19th century. One was Marlborough House, where Marmont Road is today, which was purchased in 1829 for use as a workhouse until the 1860s. Paupers from the City of London lived there until it was demolished. St Mary-le-Strand House, on the south side of the Old Kent Road, was built as a workhouse in 1811 by the parochial authorities of St Mary-le-Strand in the City of Westminster. It was used for that purpose until 1836.

Poor people also received help from charities. In 1834 the Peckham Pension Society – which exists today under the name

Peckham and Kent Road Pension Society – was founded by the
Rev Edmund Lilley. Its aim was to provide financial assistance
"without distinction of religion, sect or country, to decayed
housekeepers or their widows, of good character, residing within
the liberty of Peckham". A monthly payment of 26 shillings
was made to men and 21 shillings and eight pence to women.
The candidates "must have completed their sixtieth year, and have
contributed by direct taxation in the said liberty of Peckham for
at least seven years to the parish rates, and not have received
parochial relief for four years preceding their recommendation".
Many respectable aged and infirm people would have ended
their days in a workhouse without this assistance.

Housing was also provided by charitable organisations. In 1827
the Licensed Victuallers purchased land on which to build an
asylum, now Caroline Gardens in Asylum Road. The first stone
was laid on 29 May 1828 by His Royal Highness the Duke of
Sussex, the sixth son of George III. The building contract was
for 43 houses but demand was high and many more houses
were built over the following half-century. By the 1870s the
asylum consisted of 170 units of accommodation; 205 residents
were provided with shelter, financial help, coal, medicine and
medical advice.

Property owner Daniel Cronin built the Camden Houses which
opened in 1866 on the site where the Camden Estate was built in
the 1970s. The houses were for "twelve aged persons who,
through misfortune, have fallen into reduced circumstances".
Camden Houses were described as a "snug retreat" in "one of the
most charming little spots to be found in the parish of
Camberwell". Applicants for admission had to be 60 years of age,
and possess an income of not less than £25 nor more than £40 a
year. Residents were not allowed to receive parish relief and
unmarried men were not eligible for admission.

The Girdlers' Company built the fine almshouses in Albert (now
Consort) Road in 1834 to commemorate Cuthbert Beeston, who had
been Master of the Worshipful Company of Girdlers in 1570. Seven
houses were erected for freemen of the Company or their wives.

The Licensed Victuallers' Asylum, 1830.
Drawn by T.M. Baynes and engraved by H. Wallis.

Each received a pension in addition to the use of the house. The Girdlers' Company also opened almshouses for six pensioners in Choumert Road in 1852. These Peckham almshouses, which still exist, replaced ones in the City of London built with money bequeathed by George Palyn to the Girdlers' Company. The site was given by Thomas Watkins who was a Girdler.

The Metropolitan Beer and Wine Trade Society built an asylum, which stands on the north side of Nunhead Green, for less fortunate members of their trade. The first stone was laid by Lord Monteagle, Patron of the Society, on 9 June 1852. Seven houses were built for 13 residents. In 1872 a new wing, Albion Terrace, was added. It fronted Gordon Road and consisted of eight houses.

Blind people received help from the Surrey Association for the General Welfare of the Blind; this is now Action for Blind People based in Verney Road. The organisation was established in 1857 for

the purpose of teaching blind people to read in their own homes
and of supplying books free of charge. In 1860 the organisation
moved to premises in the High Street where goods were sold. The
Society helped poverty-stricken blind people to find employment.
They were also taught various trades without charge.

The Society for Organizing Charitable Relief and Repressing
Mendicity opened an office in Peckham in the 1870s. As begging
was a problem, this organisation performed valuable work in
helping poor people.

An Emigration Home for destitute girls was run by Maria Susan
Rye from 1869 at Avenue House, 1 Rosewall Road, Bull Yard.
Avenue House was once a family mansion of some note; it was
demolished in about 1950 to make way for the bus garage that
stood where the Safeway car park is today. Despite public
opposition, Maria Rye and her two younger sisters took to Avenue
House children aged eight to 13 who were living on the streets or
in workhouses.

At Niagara-on-the-Lake, Canada, Maria Rye acquired a building
which she called "Our Western Home". To this house Miss Rye
took the children from Peckham. After further training they were
taken to various parts of Canada to work as domestic servants for
respectable families. In 1895 Maria Rye transferred the two
institutions in Peckham and Niagara to the Church of England
Central Society for Providing Homes for Waifs and Strays, now
The Children's Society.

Lord Shaftesbury, whose memorial is Eros in Piccadilly Circus,
encouraged Maria Rye in her work and was chairman of the
Emigration Home. On 25 March 1874 he presided over the second
annual meeting of Peckham Working Boys' Home in Meeting
House Lane. This home was established by Mr J.H. Stiles, who had
been a ragged schoolboy. The home's aim was to provide shelter,
clothing, employment and a simple education for destitute boys.
The treasurer of the Boys' Home was John Taylor, of Sunbury at
Peckham Rye, whose daughter became Dame Elizabeth Cadbury.

Clean water and better drainage

Wells were the main source of water until piped supplies
gradually became available during the 19th century. The first
supply of pumped water to the parish of Camberwell can be
traced to 1804.

The Metropolis Water Act 1852 called for a constant supply of
water throughout the whole metropolitan district. In order to play
its part in achieving this, the Southwark and Vauxhall Water
Company in 1854 acquired 14 acres of land between Peckham
Rye and Nunhead Cemetery so reservoirs could be built to serve
the increasing number of people who were expected to move into
the district. Four reservoirs came into service in the 1870s.
(These were replaced by two new ones opened in 1994.) Each
reservoir was covered in accordance with the Act, which aimed to
protect water from germs and impurities in the London air.

After the inquiries that followed the disastrous cholera invasion
of London in 1849, water had to be pumped from the Thames six
miles above the Teddington Lock. An engine at Hampton Court
pumped water from the river and forced it on to Battersea where
powerful engines sent it to Nunhead. It was not until 1897 that
the Southwark and Vauxhall Water Company could assert that
every home in its district was constantly supplied with water.

Efficient house drainage and sewage disposal were amenities to
be prized, especially when it was shown that cholera was linked
to insanitary conditions. In none of the outbreaks of cholera in
London from 1832 did the parish of Camberwell escape serious
infection. In 1832-3 there were 107 deaths; in 1849, 504; in 1854,
553; in 1866, 46; and in 1867, 88.

The preamble to auction particulars of a new building estate in
the 1840s began: "Bath Road runs through the Estate and has a
Famous Sewer already constructed from one end to the other, and
there is a deep gravelly soil throughout this locality forming also a
natural drainage which, together with the mild salubrious air for

which the neighbourhood is proverbial, have gained for Peckham
its present celebrity for promoting health and longevity."
Sewerage arrangements in London suburbs before the 1850s were
casually contrived. There was no obligation on a builder of a row
of cottages or an estate to provide adequate drainage. Occupiers
of suburban dwellings therefore often had no other means of
drainage than the common ditches.

At a meeting of the newly-formed Metropolitan Commission of
Sewers in 1848 the surveyor reported on the drainage of 87
houses in Peckham. He stated that the basements, areas, yards
and gardens were overflowing with soil-drainage from adjoining
cesspools; two or three of these, each with a capacity of about 10
cubic yards, were found in and about each house. Altogether 181
cesspools were discovered and their contents were emptied into
2,384 cartloads.

Peckham was almost wholly undrained in 1856, when the reformed
Camberwell Vestry came into being with the aim of improving the
sewerage and draining, as well as maintaining or improving other
aspects of the parish such as the paving, cleansing and lighting. By
1871 Camberwell Vestry had succeeded in ensuring the abolition of
over 4,000 cesspools and the provision of an almost equivalent
number of water-closets and 50 miles of covered sewers.

Education for all

Schools run by private individuals, voluntary organisations and
churches were the only source of education prior to the 1870 act
of parliament that established state schools in London.

In the 18th and early 19th century a number of schools – often
offering boarding accommodation – were founded to provide
education for the sons of the wealthier middle classes. Peckham
Collegiate School was founded in about 1770. In the middle of the
19th century it moved to the corner of Queen's Road and Burchell
Road. College Hall, now used by a commercial firm, still exists.

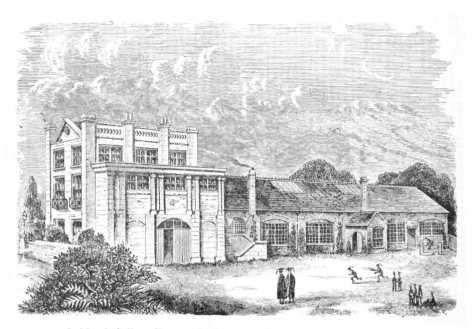

*St Mary's College, Hanover Park, a view of c.1870.
A car park now occupies the site.*

The Rev Thomas Ready and his two sisters ran a boarding school
in the High Street which was attended in the 1820s by Robert
Browning from the age of eight or nine. The school was chosen
by Browning's family as the best in the neighbourhood but
unfortunately he was miserable there. One of the poet's
biographers wrote: "Time softened the pain of the endless weekly
exile but not the intense dislike of the school." However, he
remained there until he was 14.

Manilla College, Peckham Rye, stated in its prospectus that "the
sons of gentlemen are liberally boarded and carefully instructed
in the subjects necessary to prepare them for the various public
schools, the Civil Service, legal, medical, and middle-class
examinations, as well as for professional or commercial pursuits."
The school was established in 1854, in the large house which is
now 200 Peckham Rye.

St Mary's College, Hanover Park, was a self-supporting semi-public
school. It was established in 1868 to provide at a moderate charge
a superior commercial and classical education on Church of England
principles. The school was in union with the National Society
Middle-Class School Committee. In the 1870s 260 pupils attended.

Peckham also offered establishments for the education of
teenage girls. The Manor House School used the former Basing
Manor House, close to what are now Peckham High Street and
Bellenden Road. This school began in 1854. In the 1850s a ladies'
school was set up in Myrtle House, 13 Queen's Road. This was the
former home of Sir Benjamin Collins Brodie (1783–1862), who
was attendant physician to George IV and sergeant-surgeon to
William IV and Queen Victoria. There were another two colleges
for young ladies at Peckham Rye and a boarding school in
Queen's Road, where Cherry Tree Court is today.

Ragged Schools, providing an education for some of the very
poorest children, began in the 18th century and in 1844 the
Ragged School Union was set up. One such school was run in
Lower Park Road. Peckham Girls' Ragged School was in Victoria
Place; this area was demolished when the Church Army built an
estate between Peckham High Street and Bellenden Road.
Ragged Schools were entirely free for the poorest children.

In 1808 followers of the Quaker Joseph Lancaster, who was born
in Southwark, formed the Royal Lancasterian Society to enact his
educational ideas. The organisation changed its name in 1810 to
the British and Foreign School Society. British Schools were
founded in 1812 by members of the Society of Friends in a
building in Hill Street. In 1822 the school was moved to the High
Street on the site previously occupied by Peckham Theatre (on
the south side of the High Street close to the junction with Hill
Street, now Peckham Hill Street). The Birkbeck Schools were
built on land near Willowbrook Bridge purchased in 1852. The
Lancaster or monitorial system, by which the children were
employed to teach each other, was largely used.

The National Society for the Education of the Poor in the Principles
of the Established Church was founded in 1811 to take over the

schools of the Society for the Promotion of Christian Knowledge. Peckham National Schools started in Victoria Place and moved to 136 High Street. They were supported by St Chrysostom's Church, Hill Street. Over 300 children attended in the 1870s.

St John the Evangelist Church, Goose Green, ran a National School at Troy Town. This became what today is St John's and St Clement's School, Adys Road. Christ Church ran a National School for infants in Arthur Street and another in Asylum Road. St Mary Magdalen Church had a school in Albert (now Consort) Road. This began in 1856 and today is Peckham's oldest existing school. Among the other church schools were St Francis Roman Catholic School in Lower Park Road, Peckham Wesleyan Day School in Stafford (now Staffordshire) Street and St Andrew's District School in Orchard Hill Street. The school building erected in 1867 by All Saints' Church has recently been renovated and can be seen behind the church in Blenheim Grove.

Camden Schools were started in 1813 by Camden Chapel, which stood where Voltaire flats are today in Peckham Road. The schools transferred to Sumner Road in 1845. The building they occupied is now used by the Sojourner Truth Community Association; it is of architectural merit and contains a very rare stepped classroom like a tiered lecture theatre.

The Elementary Education Act 1870 was a controversial measure, which was driven through Parliament by the Prime Minister, W.E. Gladstone, and the Act's author, W.E. Forster. It followed 40 years in which repeated attempts had been made to put an elementary education act on the statute book – they had all failed because of opposition from the Church of England and nonconformist denominations.

In 1870 more than half the children in London had no access to education. When the first election for an education authority was held on 29 November that year there was considerable excitement and the atmosphere was almost euphoric. After the London School Board was set up, plans were made to build new schools in Peckham and Nunhead so that children who had previously been unable to go to school could do so. By the turn of the century, the following schools had opened: Gloucester Road (1875), Peckham Park (1876), Sumner Road (1876), Bellenden Road (1877), Hollydale Road (1877), Reddins Road (1881), Wood's Road (1881), Lyndhurst Grove (1883) where Ainsworth Close and Cactus Close are today, Adys Road (1884), Peckham Rye (1884), Colls Road (1885), Ruby Street (1885), Ivydale Road (1892), Bird in Bush Road (1893), Peckham Central (1894) and Leo Street (1899).

Voluntary schools continued to function, but the new schools provided by the London School Board enabled all children to receive education, which became compulsory up to the age of ten under the Education Act 1880. At that age children could obtain a certificate and leave but if their record of attendances did not meet a standard they were required to stay on at school longer. Free elementary education was provided from 1891. Two years later the school-leaving age was raised to 11; in 1899 it rose to 12.

Compulsory school attendance caused a truancy problem, as many children did not like going to school. Also many parents wanted their children to be able to earn money to help families make ends meet. Despite the difficulties involved in providing compulsory elementary education, there was progress – as Stuart Maclure stated in *One Hundred Years of London Education 1870–1970:* "By the turn of the century the Board schools in their massive three-decker buildings had established solid traditions and regular habits."

Transport moves on

In 1750 the only way to reach Peckham and Nunhead or to travel out of the hamlets was on foot, on horseback or by horse-drawn coach. A coach went each day from the Cross Keys and Spread Eagle public house in the City of London to Peckham. By 1825 ten coaches ran from the City to Peckham each day, doing a total of 40 return journeys.

Horse-drawn omnibuses superseded coaches in the 1830s. They could carry more passengers and so fares were lower. The Great

Exhibition at Hyde Park in 1851 generated a lively trade and
Thomas Tilling took advantage by beginning a four-horse service
from Rye Lane to Oxford Circus. He had competitors but his
omnibuses were the fastest on the route. They ran to a strict
timetable and he called them "The Times". One is preserved in
the London Transport Museum at Covent Garden. Thomas
Tilling's grave can be seen in Nunhead Cemetery.

A Tilling omnibus, a modern reconstruction of a vehicle of the 1850s.
Thomas Tilling began running omnibuses from Peckham in 1851.
His headquarters were at Winchester House, a former grammar school
in the High Street.

Between 1835 and 1865 omnibuses were the only form of public transport available in Peckham and Nunhead. By the 1860s the omnibus had brought regular suburban travel within financial reach of the better paid clerk and artisan.

A quicker form of transport came in the 1860s when the railways arrived. Peckham Rye Station opened in 1865; in the following year other stations opened at Queen's Road, originally named Peckham, and Old Kent Road on the South London Line to London Bridge. Nunhead Station opened in 1871. The railway enabled more people to work further away from home. Although some cheap fares for workmen had been available long before the Cheap Trains Act was passed in 1883, the Act encouraged more people to travel to work by train.

Horse-trams, which superseded omnibuses because they could carry more passengers at lower fares, ran from 1871 along the Old Kent Road. The following year trams began to run along Peckham High Street and Queen's Road.

From 1826 the Peckham branch of the Grand Surrey Canal was available for transporting goods by barge to and from the Surrey Docks. This was particularly useful at a time when Peckham was fast becoming built-up. Materials for building houses, shops and other premises could be moved easily from the docks four miles away. Today the route of the canal is a linear park from Peckham Square, which is a few yards from where the canal basin was, to Burgess Park.

Towards the end of the 19th century, a growing number of people rode bicycles. Wilson's cycle firm began in Hill Street (now Peckham Hill Street) in about 1870. It opened another shop in 1882 in the High Street, where it has traded for over a century. Wilson's is now Peckham's oldest existing firm. A cycling club, The Surrey Wheelers C.C., began in Peckham. Its inaugural meeting was held in 1886; the club's headquarters were at the Hotel & Restaurant, 16 Rye Lane.

New churches, new congregations

St. Antholin's Church, Nunhead Lane, c.1905.

In 1750 Peckham's only place of worship, a nonconformist meeting house, stood at the corner of South Street, now Rye Lane, and the High Street. A new place of worship was built to replace it in 1817 and was called Hanover Chapel because of its links with the Royal House of Hanover. The Dukes of Kent and Sussex attended the opening and were not infrequent worshippers there.

As the population grew in the 19th century, new Anglican parishes were created from parent churches – in Peckham's case, St Giles, Camberwell. Peckham Chapel, opened in 1814 in Hill Street, was the first of these; it was renamed St Chrysostom's in 1865. This was followed by Christ Church, erected in 1838 next to the gasworks and replaced in 1868 by a new church south of the Old Kent Road; St Mary Magdalen, opened in 1841 in St Mary's Road on land called "the duck's nest"; St Andrew's, opened in 1865 in Glengall Road on the site of an apple orchard; All Saints', Blenheim Grove, consecrated in 1872 by Bishop Samuel Wilberforce; St Augustine's at Honor Oak, consecrated in 1873;

St Jude's, where St John's in Meeting House Lane is today, opened in 1876 after a temporary iron building had been erected to evangelise the railway construction workers; St Luke's in Pentridge Street, consecrated by the Bishop of Rochester in 1877; St Antholin's, built in 1878 in Nunhead Lane using money from Wren's St Antholin's in the City; St Saviour's in Copleston Road, paid for by tea merchant Francis Peek and opened in 1881; St Mark's, opened in 1884, where Tuke School in Woods Road is today; and All Saints', Davey Street, which was built in 1894 as a memorial to Charles Cubitt Gooch, who first started mission work in the area in 1888.

Baptists built a number of chapels including one in South Street (now Rye Lane). It was opened in 1819 but demolished to make way for the railway. The present Rye Lane Chapel opened in 1863. Lower Park Road Baptist Church, opened in 1862, was built using stone from the old Westminster Bridge in the foundations; it was later renamed Peckham Park Road Baptist Church. North Peckham Baptist Church in East Surrey Grove had its foundation stone laid by the prominent Baptist preacher C.H. Spurgeon in 1870. Nunhead Baptist Church, in what is now Gautrey Road, had foundation stones laid in 1888; the building is now used by the Emmanuel Miracle Temple of Bethany Fellowship of Great Britain. Peckham Rye Tabernacle in Nigel Road opened in 1891 and Honor Oak Baptist Church the following year. East Dulwich Baptist Church used a corrugated iron chapel in Amott Road from 1896.

Congregationalists built Peckham Rye church in Cemetery Road, now Linden Grove, in 1857; and Clifton, Asylum Road, in 1859.

Various Methodist churches were built in the 19th century. In 1865 the Wesleyans opened a church with a tall spire in Queen's Road on the site of a ladies' school, where Cherry Tree Court is today at the corner of Woods Road. The Wesleyans' former chapel, opened in 1834, was in Stafford Street and is now used by the Peckham Settlement. The United Methodist Free Churches opened chapels in Hill Street (1854) and Bellenden Road (1885); this is now Faith Chapel. Sumner Road Primitive Methodist Chapel, now Sureway International Christian Centre, was opened in 1875. The Methodist New Connexion built Waverley Park Church in Ivydale Road in 1896; it is now used by Peckham Seventh Day Adventists.

In 1866 Roman Catholics opened a large and magnificent church, the Capuchin Franciscan Church of our Lady of Seven Dolours, in what today is Friary Road. It was designed by Edward Welby Pugin and was built to serve the 3,000 Catholics who lived in the Roman Catholic District of Peckham. Many Catholics moved to the area after the potato famine in Ireland.

Unitarians opened a chapel in Avondale Road (now Rise) in 1882. Quakers built a meeting house in Hanover Street, now Highshore Road, in 1826; the front is now part of the Royal Mail Sorting Office.

Various independent chapels were built including Heaton Road (1873); Christ Church, McDermott Road (1880); and Central Hall (by 1896) in Peckham High Street. The Salvation Army opened a citadel at Nunhead Green (1891). Numerous mission halls were built and Corpus Christi College, Cambridge, opened a mission church in Canterbury (now Ilderton) Road in 1890.

The large number of churches, chapels and mission halls built in the 19th century reflected the growth in the local population and a zeal to reach the residents with the Gospel. Christians, who worked hard to enable a large number of buildings to be erected, provided social activities and practical assistance to the poverty-striken population as well as meeting spiritual needs. Nevertheless the religious census of 1851 showed that two-thirds of the population did not attend church.

Fairs, plays and other pastimes

From the late 12th century onwards, the right to hold a fair was granted by royal charter. Peckham had a fair but it is not known when it started. There is a tradition that King John killed a stag while hunting at Peckham and he was so pleased with the sport that he granted a fair lasting three weeks. Unfortunately no charter has been found to confirm this. Another tradition is that a fair was granted by Charles II, on the insistence of Nell Gwyn, when he returned from a day's sport in the neighbourhood to the residence of Sir Thomas Bond who lived in Peckham Manor House, where Peckham Hill Street is today.

The fair extended from Peckham House, where Warwick Park
School stands, to Meeting House Lane. It was held from 22 to 24
August each year. According to James Edwards, author of *London
to Brighthelmston* (1801), it was "amazingly thronged with the
lower rank of people from London".

But it was not popular with everyone. On 8 May 1823 a special
meeting of Camberwell Vestry was held to consider whether the
fairs of Peckham and Camberwell were "authorised by any grant,
charter, prescription, or other lawful and sufficient authority, in
order, if practicable, to suppress them". To keep the peace at the
fairs application was made to the Magistrate at Bow Street, in
the early part of the 19th century, for twelve officers at a cost of
five shillings a day. The fair was last held in 1827.

Though people worked long hours, a growing number of leisure
activities were available apart from those run by the increasing
number of churches. Peckham Theatre, in the High Street, was
an institution in the village. The spirited proprietor, Mr Penley of
Drury Lane notoriety, generally provided an attractive
programme. No proof has ever been found that Nell Gwyn acted
there, but a comedy in three acts was published in 1799 called
The Peckham Frolic or Nell Gwyn.

Actor John Baldwin Buckstone (1802-79) made his first
appearance in the Peckham Theatre as Captain Aubri in a
melodrama called *The Dog of Montargis*. *Hamlet* was performed
on 8 September 1807; a playbill is preserved in the Shakespeare
Memorial Library at Stratford-on-Avon. Another playbill, in
Southwark Local Studies Library, shows that *John Bull* was
performed on 31 August 1816.

The common at Peckham Rye was a popular place for recreation.
Not surprisingly, therefore, a large and enthusiastic meeting of
the principal residents was held on 7 June 1865 to consider the
best way to prevent the erection of buildings on it. It was an old
threat – Camberwell Vestry minutes dated 3 May 1766 and
14 April 1789 show that there was concern in the 18th century
about encroachments on Peckham Rye. To stop the lord of the
manor, Sir William Bowyer Smyth, allowing buildings to be

erected on Peckham Rye the manorial rights were purchased in 1868 by Camberwell Vestry. The Vestry also bought the interests of the lord of the manor in Nunhead Green and Goose Green on condition that they remained open to the public in perpetuity.

Various societies made good use of Peckham Rye. W.H. Blanch wrote in *Ye Parish of Camerwell*: "The more robust youth have a capital field for the exercise of out-door sports on the fine open space of Peckham Rye, and therefore cricket-clubs and athletic societies flourish amongst us ... the parochial authorities make every effort to promote their comfort and prosperity, and that good behaviour is the rule and not the exception amongst the multitudes that flock for recreation to this fine open space, are facts both encouraging and significant."

However, great difficulty was experienced before 1869 in keeping order on Peckham Rye and in preventing it from becoming the site of a huge fair. In 1864 32 vans of "Wombwell's wild beasts" took up residence for a while – and other invasions, more or less objectionable, were made from time to time.

A bandstand, which had been in the Royal Horticultural Society's Garden in Kensington, was moved to Peckham Rye and opened in 1889 by the Earl of Meath, chairman of the Parks and Open Spaces Committee of the London County Council. It was blown up after it had been partially destroyed by a landmine during World War II.

The common was so crowded on Saturdays and Bank Holidays that more open space was needed. After much campaigning by local people, Homestall Farm was bought with money provided by Camberwell Vestry, the London County Council and the Charity Commissioners. It was converted into Peckham Rye Park which was opened on Whit Monday, 14 May, 1894. Facilities for cricket, tennis and children's actitivies were included in the new 51-acre park.

One Tree Hill at Honor Oak was the site of an early environmental protest – a campaign to keep the wooded hillside free for the enjoyment of the general public lasted from 1896 to 1905. One Tree Hill was part of the ancient Great North Wood. At the

One Tree Hill, 1905.

beginning of the 19th century it was used as a semaphore station
by the East India Company to signal the appearance of their
vessels in the English Channel. It was also used at the time of
the threatened Napoleonic invasion of England. A cottage built
for the use of the signal operator stood at the top of the hill.

Until the autumn of 1896, when it was quietly and effectively
enclosed by a golf club, the hill had been a popular open space
that people enjoyed visiting. The erection of a six-foot fence
caused a storm of indignation. A number of meetings protesting
against the enclosure were held in 1897 on Peckham Rye.

Consequently the "Enclosure of Honor Hill Protest Committee"
was formed. The committee, which had 23 members at its first
meeting, rapidly grew to about 150.

On Sunday 10 October 1897 about 15,000 people assembled at
various points in the vicinity of the hill. Some people pulled down
part of the fence and soon the hill was covered with a disorderly
multitude. It was quickly found necessary to reinforce the police
who had been posted to keep order. An even bigger crowd of

between 50,000 and 100,000 gathered on 17 October. About 500 police, on foot and mounted, tried to keep order. Stones were thrown and a police inspector was badly wounded. After further agitation and intense campaigning, Camberwell Borough Council arranged with the London County Council for a clause to be inserted in their General Powers Bill 1902 for the compulsory acquisition of One Tree Hill. Consequently, since 1905 the hill has been freely used by members of the public.

The Peckham Young Men's Mutual Improvement Society began in 1866. Musical and elocutionary entertainment was organised and lectures on scientific and other subjects were given. The Society amalgamated with the Peckham Debating Society and later became known as the Peckham Mutual Society. Profits made at public entertainments were used for charitable purposes. These included helping sufferers of the cotton famine in Lancashire, the Barnsley Colliery Fund, the "Captain" Fund in aid of the sick and wounded soldiers in the Franco-Prussian War, the Peckham Pension Society and Peckham Girls' Ragged School. The Society had its own library and held weekly meetings in the Collyer Memorial Schools in the High Street.

Peckham Amateur Athletic Club was started in 1867. In the 1870s Peckham Annual Sports were held in Mr Bennet's field near Queen's Road Station. The first meeting of the Peckham Hare and Hounds, which developed into the Blackheath Harriers, was held on 23 October 1869 at the King's Arms, Peckham Rye. Their activities included running, jumping, steeple-chasing, hurdling, cycling and swimming. Among the other leisure organisations in the 19th century was the Peckham Amateur Orchestral Society.

As Peckham's population grew, more public houses were built to serve leisure needs. Many of the Victorian pubs still exist but not all have their original names. The Adam and Eve is now Kellie's and The Crown changed its name to Sally O'Brien's. Public houses were popular places for working men to spend their leisure time. There they were able to relax after a hard day's work. Apart from serving beer and other alcoholic drinks, some pubs provided entertainment.

Peckham Theatre of Varieties, at 263 Southampton Street (now
Way), was licensed from 1849 until 1897. Its former names were
Rosemary Branch Music Hall and Public House, People's Palace
of Varieties and Lovejoy's Music Hall. The extensive grounds
surrounding the Rosemary Branch, at the corner of what are now
Southampton Way and Commercial Way, were used for horse
racing, cricket and pigeon shooting, as well as other outdoor
sports and pastimes. A public meeting was held in June 1874 in
support of a memorial presented to Camberwell Vestry for the
preservation of the Rosemary Branch Cricket Ground as a
recreation ground, but it was not successful.

A large new public hall for musical and social occasions was
opened in Rye Lane on 1 November 1884. At the second concert
the main attraction was the singing of Lady Edward Spencer
Churchill. The building, at the rear of 164 Rye Lane, became the
Tower Cinema Annexe. Today it is used by Christ Apostolic Church.
For the energetic there was a roller skating rink at 63 Rye Lane.
The large Crown Theatre was built in the High Street, where the
closed Mecca Bingo Hall now stands; it had 2,600 seats. It opened
on 31 October 1898 and was erected on the site of a fairground.

In 1891 a Men's Institute for the Parish of St Luke was founded
in Commercial Road (now Way). It became known as St Luke's
Lads' Club and in 1911 was adopted by Bradfield College,
Berkshire. Today it is known as the Bradfield Club.

The first library in Peckham opened in the Old Kent Road on
18 October 1890; this was the gift of George Livesey, chairman of
the South Metropolitan Gas Company, to Camberwell Vestry.
The library was bombed during World War II and was replaced by
North Peckham Library in 1966. The old building was reopened
as the Livesey Museum by Sir John Betjeman on 30 March 1974.
A statue of George Livesey, which used to be in the grounds of the
gasworks, is in the Museum's Courtyard.

Camberwell Central Library in Peckham Road, next to the
Walmer Castle public house and where Kingfisher House is
today, was opened by His Royal Highness the Prince of Wales,
accompanied by the Duke and Duchess of York, on 9 October 1893.

The library was demolished after being bombed in World War II.
Nunhead Library opened in 1896 and was the gift of editor
and philanthropist John Passmore Edwards who laid the
foundation stone on 11 April 1896. There was no swimming bath
in Peckham or Nunhead in the 19th century, but residents were
able to use those at Camberwell and East Dulwich.

Rye Lane: the new high street

The High Street was Peckham's principal shopping street
until it was superseded by Rye Lane. In the late 1870s the
Metropolitan Board of Works carried out a bold scheme for
the widening of the High Street in order to provide space
for the new tram lines. All the shops on one side of the street
were demolished. As a consequence, businessmen turned
their attention to Rye Lane, which then became the main
shopping street.

The retail shop was not a Victorian invention, but the Victorian
era was the time of its most rapid growth. As Peckham and
Nunhead's population increased, particularly in the second half of
the 19th century, more shops were needed. By the end of the
1860s, Rye Lane already had a number of well-established shops
but expansion was rapid in the decades that followed.

Jones & Higgins, a drapery firm, opened at 3 Rye Lane in 1867;
within fifteen years of expansion it had subsumed a further
nine houses within its premises. In the 1890s the multiple stores
that were appearing in many parts of London put down roots in
Rye Lane. Lipton's Ltd opened at no 98 in 1891 and Dunn & Co,
hatters, established premises at no 106, replacing an oyster
merchant, in 1895. A branch of the Singer Sewing Machine Co
appeared in the same year. In 1904 one of a chain of shoe shops
named Freeman, Hardy & Willis Ltd opened. By 1907 Boots Cash
Chemists (Southern) Ltd could be found at no 20; J.Lyons & Co
Ltd were serving refreshments at no 26 from 1910 and the
following year shoesellers Stead & Simpson opened one of their
shops at no 89.

Other businesses started in various parts of Peckham and
Nunhead. Some still exist today or survived well into the 20th
century. A man from Oxfordshire, George Austin, had opened a
dairy called the Oxford Farm Dairy at 39 Brayards Road by 1876.
When the milk rounds were finished he used the milk cart for
small household removals. Billheads in the 1880s advertised
"Cows kept for infants and invalids – Milking hours 5 till 7am,
1 till 3pm." The same billheads showed an illustration of a horse-
drawn furniture van and advertised "Household Removals –
Furniture Warehoused". George Cutts set up a printing business
at 81 Bellenden Road in 1883. This was transferred to 20 Victoria
Road, now 113 Bellenden Road, in 1894. Cutts & Co Ltd closed
in 1990. Evan Cook opened a second-hand furniture shop at
72 Queen's Road in 1893. This grew into the international
transportation firm Evan Cook Limited, which is now part of the
Constantine Group.

Milton Syer, whose Hanover Works were at the corner of Rye Lane
and Hanover Street (now Highshore Road), specialised in inventing
and manufacturing sanitary equipment. One of Mr Syer's
important inventions was the "Peckham" Syphon Cistern which
was supplied to H.M.'s Board of Works and the Admiralty. This
cistern, which had no rubbers or valves to fall into disrepair, was
extremely simple and silent in its action, and had great flushing
power. It was awarded a medal at the Inventions Exhibition. The
firm closed in 1971 and the premises were demolished.

Into the metropolis

Peckham and Nunhead were originally in the parish of St Giles',
Camberwell, and it was in the old St Giles' Church that organised
local government for the Camberwell area began. On 2 June
1674, a general meeting of parishioners was held in the church
where, according to the minutes, "it was voted that a certain
number of the constant inhabitants should be nominated ...
to meet once a month in the parish church to consult with the

minister and parish officers about the affairs of the parish ...
and to communicate from time to time what they have debated of
to a general meeting of parishioners."

In common with other parishes, the committee chosen was
known as the Vestry because it originally met in the vestry of
the church. Under the Metropolis Management Act 1855 the
parish vestries were reconstituted as elected bodies and given
new powers. Vestrymen were elected by persons whose names
had been on the rate-book for a year, and eligibility for office
depended on the occupancy of premises rated at £40 or more
a year. The parish of Camberwell was divided into six wards,
each electing 12 to 18 Vestrymen.

The new Vestry was invested with powers to deal with drainage,
sanitation, paving and street lighting. Over the next few decades
it also took on new responsibilities such as the upkeep of roads
after turnpikes were abolished. Under the Representation of the
People Act 1867, Vestrymen were elected by men aged over 21
who for twelve months occupied as owner or tenant a separate
dwelling, or lodgings to the annual unfurnished value of £10.
Collectors were employed to visit every home each quarter to
collect rates to pay for services provided by the Vestry.

Another body established under the 1855 Act was the Metropolitan
Board of Works, the first metropolitan-wide local authority for
London. The Board's responsibilities in Peckham and Nunhead
related mainly to streets and sewers. Later, the Board also started
the Metropolitan Fire Brigade, exercised powers of control over
buildings, regulated places of entertainment and cleared some
slums. The Board was superseded by the London County Council
(LCC). Peckham and Nunhead were in Surrey until 1889 when
they became part of London following the creation of the LCC
under the Local Government Act 1888.

Camberwell Vestry ran most of the local government affairs in
Peckham and Nunhead until 1900 when it was replaced by the
Council of the Metropolitan Borough of Camberwell.

1900-1939:
The early twentieth century

A fluctuating population

At the end of the 19th century Peckham and Nunhead were part
of a metropolis that was growing at the rate of 100,000
inhabitants a year. The first and most fundamental stimulus to
suburban development was the remarkable fertility and rising
life expectancy of the Victorians themselves, combined with their
tendency to flock to the capital.

London was a magnet whose field of attraction included the
whole of the British Isles. A large part of its population increase
was accounted for by immigrants from the country districts and
provincial towns, and by Scottish and Irish people coming to
London in the hope of bettering themselves. Large numbers of
foreign immigrants were also drawn to the capital, particularly
from Europe. London's population grew from about 865,000 in
1801 to over 4.5 million in 1901.

The census of 1901 showed a total population of 106,826 in the
wards that approximately correspond to the area regarded today
as Peckham and Nunhead. In 1911 the figure was 105,651; in
1921 it was 107,682. Peckham's population was rising at a time of
falling numbers in other areas of inner London. It was a desirable
place to live, with a stock of decent and affordable housing and
plenty of local jobs – often in new industries. Most people enjoyed
good average earnings with only a few areas of poverty, notably
north of Peckham Road.

By 1931 Peckham's population had dropped to 99,604, but this
should be set against a background of much more dramatic falls
in other areas nearby. In this period there was a general
movement away from inner-London areas, driven both by the
growth of outer-London industries and improved transport, which
made longer-distance commuting possible for those who still
worked centrally. The new outer suburbs also gave people the
opportunity to buy, rather than rent, their home.

Grove Vale Estate, 1905.

First council estate and other buildings

When the 20th century dawned, most of the land in Peckham
suitable for building had already been used. The largest amount of
farmland still awaiting development was to the east of Grove Vale,
and here in 1901 the Metropolitan Borough of Camberwell opened
a depot for its vehicles. Next to the Grove Vale Depot the Council
built its first estate. It was empowered to do this by the Housing of
the Working Classes Act 1890. This legislation had resulted from
the Royal Commission on Housing set up in 1884, which
highlighted the need to eradicate slums. As private landlords were
largely concerned with making profit, councils became responsible
for providing decent homes. The London County Council provided
the money for Camberwell Borough Council to build this estate for
working-class people on two meadows.

Between 1903 and 1905 seven houses and 174 self-contained flats
were erected on the Grove Vale Estate. Each flat had three or
four rooms, with scullery and bath, and a separate garden for
each tenant. The flats were occupied by the more respectable and
thrifty members of the class for whom they were intended such as
the clerk or shopman. Plaques outside 106 and 129B Copleston
Road give details of the estate.

49

Peckham and Nunhead shown on the 6 inch Ordnance Survey map of 1914.

Under the Housing Act 1919, Camberwell Borough Council built the Newlands Estate in southern Nunhead in 1923. This Act imposed upon local authorities the duty of preparing housing schemes for their areas in order to build, as soon as possible, the number of houses needed to house the working classes in their districts. Each local authority was required to make a survey of its needs and report the result to the Local Government Board.

In the 1930s the London County Council started building the Friary, Oliver Goldsmith, Rye Hill and Sumner Estates. A Church Army housing estate was opened in Bellenden Road in 1933.

The County Secondary School, Peckham, now used by St James the Great Catholic Primary School, was opened in 1906 as a result of the Education Act 1902. After the building became too small and dilapidated, the school moved in 1931 to a new building opposite Peckham Rye Park and was renamed Honor Oak School; it is now used by Waverley Upper School. St. Francesca Cabrini School was built in 1930 and Hollydale Road School was rebuilt in 1931.

A few new churches and halls were built in the first few decades of the 20th century. St Saviour's opened Church House in Copleston Road in 1902. Also in the same year Nunhead Christian Band opened a hall in Nunhead Grove. St Silas', in Ivydale Road, was consecrated in 1903 to meet the needs of the residents on the recently built Waverley Park Estate. In the same year St Andrew's Mission Church was built in Waghorn Street. This is now Francis Bacon Lodge and is used by members of the mystical brotherhood of the Rosicrucians. St Paul's Church was opened in Consort Road in 1907.

Roman Catholics opened two churches - St James the Great in Elm Grove in 1904 and St Thomas the Apostle in Hollydale Road the following year. The money to build the churches was given by Miss Frances Elizabeth Ellis, who wanted the sizeable Roman Catholic population to be able to attend Mass.

Orchard Mission, in what is now Mission Place off Peckham High Street, was opened in 1906 by C. Goddard Clarke, MP. It was erected by the Ragged School Union, now the Shaftesbury Society.

The Amalgamated Society of Engineers opened its newly-built
headquarters in Peckham Road in 1901; the premises were
extended in 1916 when three buildings were linked together.

Samuel Jones opened a gummed paper factory in 1920 in
Peckham Grove – an example of the increasing industrialisation
of the area. It had a large Camberwell Beauty butterfly at the top
as this was the firm's trademark from 1912. The butterfly, made
with tiles, was moved to the former public baths and laundry in
Wells Way after the factory was demolished.

Overlooking Peckham Rye, Roberts' Capsule Stopper Co Ltd built
a striking art deco factory in 1931. It was designed by Wallis Gilbert
and Partners, architects of the London Transport bus garage in
Peckham High Street, opened in 1951, as well as the Firestone
building in Brentford and the Hoover Building at Perivale.

The Royal Arsenal Co-operative Society opened Co-operative
House on 12 October 1932. The Old Nun's Head at Nunhead
Green was replaced with the present pub in 1934 and a new
indoor market was built in Rye Lane in 1939.

Trams, trains and buses

In 1900 Peckham and Nunhead were served by steam trains
from four stations – Peckham Rye, Queen's Road, Old Kent Road
and Hatcham, and Nunhead. Horse trams dominated the Old
Kent Road, Queen's Road and the High Street. Horse buses ran
along roads with no tramlines. Horses and carts carried goods.
Hansom cabs conveyed passengers who could afford to use them;
the minimum fare was one shilling. People rode bicycles but a
motorcar was a rare sight. Barges plied up and down the
Peckham branch of the Grand Surrey Canal.

Changes came quickly. The last horse tram in Peckham ran in
1904; that year electric trams were introduced by the London
County Council on routes along the Old Kent Road and the High
Street. Trams reached Peckham Rye in 1907, with a branch from
Goose Green to a terminus at Stuart Road. A disused tram

shelter dating from 1920 still stands at the corner of Homestall Road and Cheltenham Road.

In an attempt to woo passengers away from the new electric trams, omnibus proprietors Thomas Tilling Limited introduced their first double-decker motor omnibus in 1904. Progress had been made on developing motor buses after the Locomotives on Highways Act 1896 was passed. This repealed the Locomotives Act 1865, which required a man bearing a red flag to precede every self-propelled vehicle on the public highway. The Motor Car Act 1903 raised the speed limit for 3-ton vehicles to 20 mph. The motor bus introduced by Tilling's in 1904 used the same route to Oxford Circus that was travelled by their "Times" omnibuses from 1851.

As the use of motor buses increased, so horse buses declined in popularity. The last London horse bus to run in regular service was one belonging to Tilling's. It made its last journey, from Peckham Rye Station to Honor Oak Tavern, on 4 August 1914. The horses then took on a new role of transporting soldiers in World War I.

Peckham High Street c.1910. Note the motorcar and Wilson's cycle shop.

Steam trains also lost passengers to the electric trams so the London, Brighton & South Coast Railway began to electrify the whole of its system. The South London Line was the first to be converted for use by electric trains because it was one of the company's busiest suburban lines. Public service began in 1909 and three years later the whole of the network ran electrically. Many other lines in south-east London were not electrified until the 1920s.

In 1911 the National Steam Car Company opened a garage at 20-26 Nunhead Lane. Owing to the rising cost of paraffin, steam buses ceased to run in 1919.

Old Kent Road and Hatcham Station closed temporarily in 1917, but never reopened. The former entrances can still be seen close to the railway bridge that crosses the Old Kent Road. Nunhead Station was rebuilt on the other side of Gibbon Road in 1925, when its line was electrified.

Motorcars were an unusual sight when the 20th century began and their use grew only slowly because most people could not afford to buy one. However, as the number of cars gradually increased more garages were built to sell petrol and carry out repairs. Among the motor firms operating in 1935 were Burke's Motors at 172 Queen's Road, Brittain's Petrol Stations Ltd at 133 Hill Street, The Anchor Garage at 10 Evelina Road with works in Seldon Road, and K.C. Robinson at 139 Peckham Road. Robinson was also a cycle and motor cycle specialist. Before World War II began, more cars were seen on Peckham and Nunhead roads.

One local business that took advantage of developments in motorised transport was Evan Cook Limited, a removals firm based in Queen's Road. By the time mechanised transport began to be developed, there were 30 horses in the Evan Cook stable but in 1908 every penny of the family's resources was invested in a steam wagon. The firm's fleet of vehicles grew and some were used to transport cars to docks after they had been packed into crates prior to being exported.

Providing for the public

At the beginning of the 20th century a number of public bodies provided services in the Peckham area. These included the London County Council, the London School Board and Camberwell Board of Guardians. In 1900 came a major change in the structure of local government when the Metropolitan Borough of Camberwell superseded the Camberwell Vestry. It was created as one of 28 metropolitan boroughs under the London Goverment Act 1899. Each had its own mayor, aldermen and elected councillors. In their early days the borough councils were primarily street and local sanitary authorities, but they later acquired wider powers, particularly in the fields of housing and social welfare.

The borough was subdivided into smaller areas – or wards. Eight of these – Clifton, Goldsmith, North Peckham, Nunhead, Rye Lane, St John's, St Mary's and The Rye – represent modern Peckham and Nunhead.

The new Council continued to use the Vestry Hall at the corner of Peckham Road and Havil Street but renamed it the Town Hall. It was rebuilt in 1934; the new section enclosed the Vestry Hall that had been erected in 1872–3. The Council Meetings of the London Borough of Southwark are held in the Council Chamber of the former Vestry Hall.

Camberwell Vestry bought land in Lewisham for future use as a burial ground. When the metropolitan boroughs were created in 1900, boundaries were changed so the land where Camberwell New Cemetery was opened in Brenchley Gardens in 1927 was in Camberwell. To compensate Lewisham for its loss, Camberwell's land to the south of Honor Oak Station was transferred to Lewisham. Under the Cremation Act 1902, the Metropolitan Borough of Camberwell opened Honor Oak Crematorium and Garden of Remembrance in 1939. Lord Horder, an eminent physician, performed the opening ceremony.

Honor Oak Crematorium shortly after its opening in 1939.

Operating in parallel with the Metropolitan Borough of
Camberwell was the London County Council. From 1904 the LCC
was responsible for schools. This followed the abolition of the
London School Board under the Education Act 1903. Parks,
including Peckham Rye Park, were also under the control of the
LCC. Half the cost of Leyton Square Garden was paid by the
LCC. The garden was laid out by the Metropolitan Public
Gardens Association and opened in 1901; it was later extended
and is protected by the London Squares Preservation Act 1931.

The LCC ran the fire service. A new Fire Station was opened in
Peckham Road on 9 July 1925 by Geoffrey Head, chairman of the
LCC Fire Brigade Committee. It was the first in London built to
meet the requirements of shift working.

As there was a need for better water supplies, a new reservoir
was built. Four hundred men spent three years constructing the
Beachcroft Reservoir, the largest brick-built underground
reservoir in Europe. It was named after Sir Melvill Beachcroft,
the first chairman of the Metropolitan Water Board. The nineteen
million bricks used in building it were made from clay excavated
on site. It was officially opened in 1909 by the Lord Mayor of
London, Sir George Wyatt Truscott. The reservoir was built on
cricket grounds and houses were erected on much of the
remaining land. Homestall Playing Fields are all that remains of
a much larger sports ground where Jack Hobbs, the Surrey and
England cricketer, played for the Honor Oak Cricket and Lawn
Tennis Club in 1920.

The Camberwell Board of Guardians was responsible for helping
poor people by providing workhouses, infirmaries, dispensaries
for treatment and residential schools. A Relief Station, where
poor people received assistance, was opened in 1901 in Albert
(now Consort) Road. This later became an LCC Welfare Clinic
and is now Consort Road Clinic run by Optimum Health Services.

Under the Local Goverment Act 1929, the Poor Law Union was
abolished, workhouses were closed and the LCC took over the duties
of the Camberwell Board of Guardians from the following year. In
addition, the Act authorised the LCC to provide health and welfare
services other than by way of the poor law. The Council could
therefore provide medical treatment for everyone, irrespective of the
patient's financial condition. Local people were able to use St Giles'
Hospital and other former institutions run by the Camberwell
Board of Guardians. In addition, orphans were cared for under the
education system instead of by way of poor-relief.

Whilst the majority of Peckham residents enjoyed a respectable –
if not spectacular – standard of living, a minority lived in or close
to poverty. Most attempted to deal with the problem as best they
could, but at the height of the depression in 1931 a small number
of residents of the Oliver Goldsmith Estate rebelled. The group,
who were threatened with eviction for non-payment of rates,
banded together to resist the actions of sheriffs' officers. At one
stage more than 50 men were imprisoned for non-payment; many

others, despite dire poverty, were threatened with jail.
The problems caused by the high levels of unemployment in the
1930s were highlighted in a moving feature in *Picture Post* on
21 January 1939, which pictured a typical day in the life of a
Peckham man who struggled to provide basic necessities for his
family and walked miles in a fruitless search for work.

As there were many poor people living in Peckham and Nunhead,
voluntary organisations had an important role in the community.
Pitt Street Settlement was founded by Charles Lisle Watson
(1890-1970). He became a Sunday School teacher at Camden
Chapel in 1908 and became aware of the poverty and deprivation.
In order to help boys who were in need of moral and spiritual
support, he took rooms in Pitt Street and organised activities for
them. He started a scout troop in 1910 and the boys took part in
physical training, sport, swimming, boxing and camping. After
meeting in various halls, he obtained full-time use of a cowshed
at 43/44a Pitt Street. This site became the base of the Settlement
which developed various activities and provided help and advice
to the local community. Lisle Watson was warden for most of his
life. The Settlement closed in 1994.

The Union of Girls' Schools for Social Service, which had started in
1897 and was supported by girls' public schools, moved its offices to
Stafford (now Staffordshire) Street in 1931. The new premises were
opened by Queen Mary. The Settlement provided help to many
needy local people. One of the contributors to *The Times of our
Lives: Growing up in the Southwark area 1900-1945* wrote: "The
good ladies from the Settlement used to visit the old and sick and
bring them warm petticoats and flannel drawers to keep them
warm." Second-hand clothes were sold very cheaply twice a week so
that families had more unemployment pay left over for food. The
Settlement started a nursery school in 1935 which chose the name
Nell Gwyn and in 1994 moved into a former LCC school building in
Meeting House Lane. The UGS is known today as The Peckham
Settlement and continues to do valuable work. It is aiming to raise
a million pounds so new premises can be built which are suitable for
serving local people in the 21st century.

Cinema, sports and parks

In the early part of the 20th century, as the music hall declined, cinemas spread. Some were converted from existing buildings, others – usually extremely opulent – were purpose-built. The cinema proved as popular in Peckham as it did elsewhere.

The Peckham Picture Playhouse used the former Hanover Chapel after the Congregationalists moved out in 1910. It stood opposite Jones and Higgins' store at the corner of Rye Lane and the High Street; it was demolished in 1914. The Crown Theatre in the High Street became a cinema after 1912 and was called the Peckham Hippodrome Picture Palace. After being demolished, it was replaced by the Gaumont Palace Cinema, which opened in 1932. This was the first Gaumont Palace in London erected by the Gaumont-British Picture Corporation.

The impressive Tower Cinema was opened by the actress Gladys Cooper at 116 Rye Lane on 19 November 1914. The Astoria cinema opened in 1930 in the Old Kent Road close to Canal Bridge. It had 2,600 seats. The Odeon opened in 1938 in Peckham High Street with 2,100 seats; it was built on the site of Queen's Picture Theatre, which was established by 1911. There were also other cinemas including the Tower Cinema Annexe, which used the former public hall at 164 Rye Lane and the Imperial Play House at 56 and 58 Rye Lane. Marks & Spencer opened a shop on the site on 23 November 1934. The Regal cinema occupied a site at the junction of the Old Kent Road and Gervase Street.

The waiting room at Peckham Rye Station was converted in November 1921 into a billiard saloon for the neighbourhood.

On Peckham Rye, next to a pond where boating was a popular pastime, the London County Council opened a lido, without ceremony, on 8 September 1923. Wilson's Rendezvous was situated on the east side of Peckham Rye adjacent to Nunhead Crescent opposite the lido. It was pictured on the front page of

The Peckham Picture Playhouse, c.1911.
The cinema occupied the former Hanover Chapel.

The World's Fair on 4 July 1936 when it was described as "a popular London fair ground". William Wilson, who ran it, was one of the pioneers of the Showmen's Guild. He died in 1951 and the following year the London County Council bought the site so that Creed House could be built on it.

Another popular leisure activity was football. Nunhead Football Club, formerly known as Wingfield House, was founded as a club for working boys by a number of gentlemen connected with the Stock Exchange. After various changes, the team in 1907 moved to Brown's Ground, St Asaph Road. Nunhead FC was one of the strongest clubs in the Isthmian League from 1908 until 1939. When Dulwich Hamlet FC opened a new ground at Dog Kennel Hill in October 1931, Nunhead were the first opponents. A crowd of 16,254 watched a 1-1 draw. The Club folded in 1942 after its benefactor's timber firm was destroyed in the Blitz. The ground is now Haberdashers' Askes' Hatcham College playing fields.

The need for open spaces where people could relax by walking or sitting in pleasant surroundings was recognised by Camberwell Borough Council who opened Brenchley Gardens in 1928. The Gardens were named after Alderman William Brenchley and were created on land occupied by allotments. The gardens were extended after the adjacent railway tracks were lifted following the closure of the line from Nunhead to Crystal Palace High Level Station in 1954.

World War I: Thousands volunteer

In the first two years of World War I, more than 100,000 young men joined up at the Camberwell Town Hall, the chief recruiting station for South London. More than 4,000 were officers and men recruited for Camberwell's own Gun Brigade, the 33rd (Camberwell) Divisional Artillery. Proudly they toured the local streets, led by their mounted band, before setting off for the Somme, Arras and Passchendaele. An impressive War Memorial in Camberwell Old Cemetery, in Forest Hill Road, records the names of the local men who were killed in action.

During the war, the basement of the Tower Cinema in Rye Lane was an official air raid shelter. There was another shelter between Goldsmith Road and Frankton Road. The basement of a brewery in Hill Street was also used as a shelter.

Women fuelling the furnaces in the South Metropolitan Gas Works during World War I. About 3,000 women were employed at the gasworks.

Tilling's garage in Bull Yard became a shell-case factory and 3,000 women worked in the South Metropolitan Gas Works in the Old Kent Road. Putting coal in the retorts in the gasworks was a very hot and back-breaking job for the women.

In 1916 a naval gun with a six-inch diameter bore was mounted on One Tree Hill to counter the threat of Zeppelin airships. It was used only once – the shell was projected vertically and missed its target. Unfortunately, it landed on the west side of Peckham Rye and destroyed part of the tramway. The remains of the gun emplacement can still be seen at the summit of One Tree Hill.

In *"Even such is time" – The Air Raids on London 1915-1918*, John Hook recorded that an incendiary bomb fell in Peckham Rye Park in 1917. In February 1918 a bomb dropped in Pennethorne Road, injuring two men and a woman. Another bomb fell 300 yards from Nunhead Station. Clifton Congregational Church in Asylum Road suffered air raid damage.

After raids, boy scouts went around on their bicycles shouting the "all clear". Prisoners of war lived in huts on Peckham Rye.

In *The Times of our Lives: Growing up in the Southwark area 1900-1945,* Dick Piper recalled his experiences by saying: "I was almost six years old when the 1914 war broke out. The days that followed seem at this late stage to be composed of school and food shortages and the nights of fear during the air raids.

"At the outbreak of war we had a small sweet and tobacconist's shop in Sumner Road, Peckham, and here it was that I experienced my first air raids. I would crouch in the recess by the side of the fireplace in the kitchen and remain as quiet as a mouse until the all clear. One bad time was when an aerial torpedo seemed to pass overhead with a terrible rattling noise. It dropped in Albany Road near the Old Kent Road and did a lot of damage, causing many deaths.

"The air raids were announced by police riding round on bicycles with placards on their chests, blowing whistles and shouting 'Take cover'. Later we had the maroons. The Zeppelins were the first raiders. I saw one come down in flames. It was brought down at Potters Bar. Men would climb the lamp posts and smash the gas lights, although generally the blackout was not so strictly enforced as in the Second World War.

"Meat, I believe, was rationed except that if you had the money, a bit extra could always be found. I used to have to queue for potatoes and a pail of coal, sometimes without success, as often the supply was exhausted before my turn came. We sometimes obtained what we called 'haddock's ears' from the local smoke hole (fish shop) and a piece of hard cheese from the provision merchant to augment our meagre food supply.

"German tradesmen, many of whom must have been here for years, were badly treated and I remember a German baker near us in Rosemary Road having a brick thrown through his window.

"Apart from the shortages, the air raids and the occasional wounded soldier in his blue hospital clothes, the war was very remote to us children; or, perhaps, because we were young, we didn't understand the terrible tragedy that was being enacted as the adults did."

A famous health experiment

Dr George Scott Williamson (1884–1953) and Dr Innes Pearse
(1889–1978), who were engaged in research at the Royal Free
Hospital in London, wanted to discover how to enable people
to be responsible for their own and their families' health.
The two doctors and their colleagues decided to offer a health
service in the form of a family club to all the families living in
a selected area of London who were willing to pay a small
membership subscription.

A search was made for an area of London with families who
were handicapped neither by extreme poverty nor by being
supported on a pedestal of servants and bound by upper-class
social conventions. Within these limits, they wanted as much
variety of income levels and occupations as possible.

No part of central London seemed suitable so the two doctors
approached the Medical Officer of Health for the Metropolitan
Borough of Camberwell with their plans. He said: "There is
little provision for infant welfare in the borough. If you will
be doing that, I shall be only too pleased to have you. Whatever
else you do is nothing to do with me." They told him that they
were scientists hoping to find out how people living under modern
industrial conditions of life might best cultivate health, and their
research would therefore benefit humankind as a whole.

Dr Williamson and Dr Pearse asked him if he could recommend
a fairly densely populated area of the borough in which there
were few unemployed or casual labourers, so that families would
be reasonably well nourished. He told them of a part of Peckham
that housed mainly steadily employed artisans (skilled and semi-
skilled workers and self-employed craftsmen), clerical workers,
small businessmen and tradesmen.

In April 1926 they took a small double-fronted house with a
garden at 142 Queen's Road and furnished it with a kitchen,
clubroom, consulting and changing rooms, children's playroom
and, later, a bathroom. They circulated all households within easy
walking – or pram-pushing – distance of the club, which they

142 Queen's Road, the first home of the Pioneer Health Centre.

called The Pioneer Health Centre, having been forestalled by a food store in their first choice of name - The Health Centre.

They explained that the club was not a treatment centre but was concerned with promoting health, detecting the beginnings of disease and giving advice on how to obtain necessary treatment. There were only two conditions of membership: families must pay a subscription of 6d a week and every family member must agree to undergo a periodic medical examination.

The Pioneer Health Centre building in St Mary's Road which opened in 1935.

Dr Williamson and Dr Pearse were investigating health. They had chosen an area in which they expected to find relatively healthy people but what they found instead was sickness. They wrote: "Of parents over 25 years of age examined by us, we were greatly astonished to find that for all without exception there was something to be done and that in many there was frank disease."

By 1929 it was plain that the premises were quite inadequate for a family health club. The decision was therefore taken to close the first Pioneer Health Centre that year and to design and collect funds for a new and purpose-built centre. In 1931 the Pioneer Health Centre became registered with the Board of Charity Commissioners for England and Wales as "a company

not having a share capital and limited by guarantee". Money
was slow to come in because the economic slump was at its
height; this caused the committee of the Pioneer Health Centre
Ltd some anxiety. Then Jack Donaldson (later Lord Donaldson of
Kingsbridge) joined the group and soon afterwards transferred
£10,000 of the £22,000 he had inherited from his father to the
account of the Pioneer Health Centre. This generous action
inspired others to give on a larger scale than before, and another
£10,000 was immediately subscribed. They then had enough
money for the building that Scott Williamson had planned. When
a site in St Mary's Road was made available to them, they
decided to go ahead and erect it, while continuing to seek funds
to cover the costs of running the club as membership was
building up. Lord Nuffield contributed generously at this time.

After six years of planning and the raising of private funds, the new
Pioneer Health Centre was built in St Mary's Road and opened on
3 May 1935. The building was designed by Sir E. Owen Williams to
fulfil the requirements laid down by Dr Scott Williamson for the
experiment. Its total costs, with basic equipment, was £38,000. It
was described by one of the leading architects of the time, Walter
Gropius, as "an oasis of glass in a desert of brick". The building is
now listed grade II* and is being converted into flats.

In *The King's England: London,* Arthur Mee wrote: "One of the
most interesting of all Peckham's buildings is its remarkable
Health Centre, a high structure with glass walls, looking like a
fine modern factory set in an orchard. It is a great clubhouse for
the families of Peckham, where they find every encouragement
known to science to be healthy and happy, and wise. Here they
may dance, fence, play games, enjoy physical exercises and swim
in a beautiful blue-green bath. There is a children's playground, a
library, a cafeteria, a kitchen, a hall and a running-track. There is
room for 2000 members.

"In setting up this great Health Centre Peckham has set a fine
example to the densely peopled areas of our great cities. The West
End of London has nothing to equal it. In this modern building this
pioneer centre is establishing a healthy community of families; it is
a great Family Club with its face set toward Fitness and Joy."

The families were free to use the Centre as they wished, individually and collectively. They developed and followed a wide range of interests and activities. Each member of the family was given a thorough medical examination, known as a health overhaul, and the findings were communicated at the family consultation. A year after opening, health levels had measurably improved. This was maintained, together with excellent growth and development of the babies, children and adolescents.

In 1935 Dr Pearse rented Oakley House at Bromley Common. Several members of the staff lodged in the house. On the 77 acres around it a herd of Jersey cows was pastured and preparations were made to grow organic vegetables and fruit. The two doctors found that the vegetables on sale in the Peckham shops were frequently stale and the milk was either pasteurised or unsafe. Tuberculin-tested milk was prohibitively expensive. Within a year of acquiring Oakley House, raw milk from the tuberculin-tested Jersey herd was on sale in the Centre at the current price of ordinary milk in Peckham. Vegetables and fruit were grown on the farm and sold in the Centre's cafeteria.

Much valuable work was done with hundreds of families until World War II. The war immediately broke up the families and it was considered too dangerous for large numbers of people to be congregated near the London docks in a building largely made of glass. The Centre reopened after the war.

1939-1945:
World War II causes devastation

Attacks by massed enemy bombers and later unmanned flying
bombs brought civilians face to face with fear, destruction and
death in a new way during World War II. The first few months
after the outbreak of war were quiet, with few enemy attacks. But
in September 1940 began the sustained onslaught of bombing
attacks that lasted well into the following year and became known
as the Blitz. For the two years after this, attacks were considerably
fewer and life much quieter but from mid-1944 to the end of the
war Londoners lived in daily fear of the V1 and V2 flying bombs
that came singly and out of the blue rather than as part of a raid.
In November 1944 a V2 hit Peckham and killed nine people.

This intensely destructive war placed new and very great
demands on the resources of local government. The metropolitan
boroughs were responsible for civil defence – including the provision
of air-raid shelters. They also had to perform salvage operations
after air raids and lay on first-aid facilities for the wounded.

In 1939 air-raid shelters for 672 people were built under
Peckham Rye, where the hard surface is today opposite the
former Kings on the Rye.

Plans for evacuation were drawn up by the Ministry of Health
and the Board of Education, assisted by the London County
Council. Families were split up. Fathers were enlisted in the
armed services and many children were evacuated. Women found
themselves doing jobs normally done by men.

Morrison shelters were put in people's homes and Anderson
shelters erected in people's gardens. Adys Road School, now used
by St John's and St Clement's School, was an auxiliary fire
station and there were fire sub-stations at Colls Road LCC
School, Holdron's in Rye Lane, Honor Oak School and the London
Passenger Transport Garage in Nunhead Lane.

Stretcher Party Depots were based in the LCC schools in Leo
Street and Southampton Way, St Paul's church hall in Consort
Road, the Congregational church hall in Bellenden Road and in

Bomb damage at Hanover Park; 17-18 January 1943.

St Silas' church hall, Inverton Road. First-Aid Posts were in the
Bird-in-Bush Welfare Centre at 616 Old Kent Road, the LCC
School Treatment Centre at 7 Hanover Park and St Anthony's
Infant Welfare Centre, 22 Linden Grove. The District Air Raid
Warden's Office was at 123 Queen's Road. There were 18 Group
Warden's Posts in various parts of Peckham and Nunhead.

The Metropolitan Borough of Camberwell, which included
Peckham and Nunhead, was the fourth most heavily damaged
borough in London. Bomb damage affected 90 per cent of its
houses – and a similar proportion of its public and commercial
buildings. Most churches in SE15 were bombed. More than 1,000
residents of the borough lost their lives in air raids; more than
5,000 were seriously injured.

In 1940, 11 people were killed when a bomb hit the King's Arms
at Peckham Rye. In the same year the former Tilling's Bull Yard
depot was bombed and a fleet of London Transport private-hire
coaches was destroyed.

In September 1940 the Odeon Cinema remained open during a
seven-hour air raid warning. The usherettes sang, danced and led
the audience in community singing "and generally provided an
entertainment to pass the hours pleasantly".

Allotments were created in Peckham Rye Park and a Barrage
Balloon Unit was based in the park. Hay crops were cultivated on
Peckham Rye and were harvested by the park-keepers. Four
years after the end of the war, *The Advertiser* on 8 June 1949
showed a tractor harvesting hay on the Rye. Huts on the Rye,
four of which still exist, were used at different times for housing
Italian and German prisoners of war and later Polish refugees.

1945-2000: Modern times

Flats replace Victorian houses

The heavy bombing of World War II accelerated the pre-war programme of slum clearance. But it also damaged or destroyed many Victorian houses that would, with improvement, have been adequate for continued occupation. Some of the houses could be repaired but many had to be replaced. A massive rebuilding programme was launched, and blocks of flats rose on land previously occupied by Victorian terraces. Meanwhile, numerous "prefabs" were erected on sites cleared of bomb damage and many survived for much longer than originally planned.

The London County Council built the Linden Grove and Peckham Park Estates in the 1940s. In the next decade the LCC extended the Friary and Oliver Goldsmith Estates and built the Heaton Road, Lindley and Nunhead Estates. After the war, the LCC also extended the Rye Hill and Sumner Estates which had been started in the 1930s. Camberwell Borough Council built the East Dulwich Road Estate in the 1950s and also built many other properties where bombs had dropped. In the 1960s Camberwell Borough Council built the Acorn, Atwell, Brayards and Pelican Estates before it was superseded in 1965 by Southwark Council.

The Greater London Council (GLC) – until it was abolished in 1986 – continued the building programme started by the LCC and erected Bells Gardens, Clifton, Gloucester Grove, Ledbury, Tappesfield, Tustin, Unwin and Willowbrook Estates. High-rise blocks on the Ledbury Estate were made from prefabricated slabs that were bolted together on site. This was quicker than using bricks. Southwark Council built Barset, Brimmington, Camden, Consort, Cossall, Limes Walk, Moncrieff, New James and North Peckham Estates. Most residents of these estates were tenants of the local authority whereas before World War II the great majority of people who did not own their homes were tenants of private landlords.

The scale of the post-war housing programme was huge, driven by government grants and high demand. Homes had to be built as quickly as possible because so many people needed accommodation. Camberwell had more new homes built than any other London borough.

The Linden Grove Estate.

Some of the new developments were themselves vast. For instance, the Gloucester Grove, North Peckham and Camden Estates formed one huge area of concrete council housing. Tenants who initially welcomed new facilities such as indoor toilets soon found drawbacks to the design – access to shops was not easy and the estates' long concrete walkways seemed to foster crime. The estates declined sharply in popularity.

Residential homes for elderly people were built in 1969 at Livesey, Tustin Street, and in 1971 at Ammon, Sumner Road. In addition, sheltered accommodation was provided at Asylum Road, Barset, Consort, Cossall, D'Eynsford, Jack Jones House, Linden Grove, North Peckham and Russell Court. Other accommodation was erected by organisations such as the Camberwell Housing Society, which built flats at Troy Town in 1952.

After the Housing Act 1974 was passed, an increasing amount of accommodation was provided by Housing Associations. Hyde converted the former workhouse, known as The Spike, into flats; it also owns much other property in SE15. Bishop Wilfred Wood Close was built for the African Refugee Housing Action Group; it was named after a former Archdeacon of Southwark who became

Bishop of Croydon. Habinteg built accommodation for disabled
people in Barset Road. London's first Habitat for Humanity
homes are being built in Gordon Road.

In the 1980s there was much concern about the social problems
on some of the post-war estates, particularly in North Peckham.
Living conditions created feelings of hopelessness, frustration and
despair. Flats needed repairing, the environment was neglected,
there were high levels of crime and people felt isolated. There
were large numbers of unemployed people living in high-density
housing. Riots erupted in Peckham in 1985 and a shop at 103
Peckham High Street was burnt out.

The Government recognised in the 1990s that a large part of
Peckham needed to be rebuilt. The Peckham Partnership was
therefore set up with the task of demolishing five estates in
North Peckham (Camden, Gloucester Grove, North Peckham,
Sumner and Willowbrook) and replacing the estates with terraced
houses and gardens built by Southwark Council, housing
associations and private developers. The seven-year programme
costing £270 million began in 1995. It is the biggest urban
regeneration programme of its type in London.

New streets have given opportunities to honour former residents.
Councillor Charles Coveney, microbiologist Walter Finch and
Dr Harold Moody are among the people to be commemorated by
having a street named after them.

Self-build houses were erected in Timberland Close in 1995.
The name was taken from the timber that was carried by barge
on the Peckham branch of the Grand Surrey Canal.

Progress in providing accommodation for homeless and rootless
people was highlighted when Joe Richards House, 100 Queen's
Road, was opened in 1998 by Harriet Harman, MP for Camberwell
and Peckham. Each resident was provided with a pleasant single
room, in sharp contrast to the gaunt dormitories in The Spike, and
given access to a wide range of services for rehabilitation.

There are some pockets of Victorian housing that remain in good
condition, notably in Nunhead; but much of the terraced housing in

Peckham needs to be renovated and modernised. A ten-year
programme in the Bellenden Renewal Area began in 1997. Not only
will Victorian housing be improved, but so will the environment.

From canal barges to Eurostar

Electric trams were phased out and replaced by buses,
which were far more flexible than trams because no rails
were needed. After the last tram ran in 1952, motor buses
provided most of the local public transport by road.

A bus garage was built on the site of Tilling's Bull Yard
depot which had been bombed. Peckham Garage was opened
in 1951 and was London Transport's first post-war garage.
The 52,800 square foot parking area was roofed in reinforced
concrete to the latest "barrel" design, the first of its kind
in London. The bus garage was demolished in 1995-6 to
make way for an extension to the Safeway store in The
Aylesham Centre.

In 1954 the last train ran from Nunhead to Crystal Palace
High Level Station due to a decline in the number of rail
passengers on this local line. Another major change in rail
transport occurred 40 years later when long-distance Eurostar
trains began running through Peckham to the Channel Tunnel.

Barge transport along the Peckham branch of the Grand Surrey
Canal ceased in 1971 following the closure of the Surrey Docks.
The Thames was too shallow for the huge ships carrying cargo
containers, so Tilbury became London's main port. A linear park
was created by filling in the canal and landscaping it – so linking
the heart of Peckham with Burgess Park.

An increasing percentage of London's population became car
owners as affluence increased after the war, and local roads became
more congested with cars. In addition, there was a growth in the
volume of goods carried in lorries partly as a result of the railway
network being drastically cut following the Beeching Report of
1963. In an attempt to cope with congested roads, a growing

number of parking restrictions were introduced and the Old Kent
Road was widened. Southwark Council is committed to
encouraging greater use of public transport and reducing the use
of private cars so air quality can be improved.

People come from around the globe

In *No Side Effects,* his third book detailing experiences as a
Peckham GP for over 40 years, Dr Isidore Crown wrote that when
he started his practice in 1953 few black people lived in Peckham.
Some had come to England on the "Empire Windrush" in 1948
and one of them, Sam King, became Southwark's first black
Mayor. His experiences and struggles are detailed in his
autobiography *Climbing up the Rough Side of the Mountain.*

As Britain needed people to work in hospitals and for London
Transport, recruitment drives were held in the West Indies.
An increasing number of Caribbean people became Peckham
residents, but limited accommodation was available within
travelling distance of jobs. Since World War II people have come
from West Africa, Turkey, Vietnam, the Indian sub-continent and
elsewhere to make a new life in Southwark.

Despite these immigrants, Peckham and Nunhead's population
still fell, from 73,894 in 1951 to 66,499 in 1961 and 63,561 in
1971. There was therefore a much bigger turnover of population
than is first apparent. Many pre-war residents moved away
during evacuation. Others, inspired by the possibility of owning
their own home (as opposed to being a local authority or private
tenant) followed them, typically to outer-London or to one of the
new towns. On the other hand, the area was attractive to
immigrants due to its proximity to work and the availability of
rented accommodation.

In *Roots of the Future: Ethnic Diversity in the Making of Britain,*
reference is made to Arundel Moody, who became the first black
British commissioned officer when he was made a lieutenant in
the Royal West Kent Regiment. He is also included in *Black
Londoners* 1880-1990 by Susan Okokon. She writes, too, about his

Picture from Negro Victory by David A. Vaughn, courtesy of The United Reformed Church

Dr Harold Moody.

brothers Dr Harold Ernest Moody, who won gold medals at the
1950 Empire Games, and Garth who became a Congregational
Minister, and his sister Dr Christine Moody who was a pioneer in
the early days of the United Nations World Health Organisation.
The father of these very talented people was Dr Harold Moody,
who came from Jamaica in 1904 to study medicine at King's
College. After qualifying as a doctor in 1913, he set up in practice
at 111 King's Road (now King's Grove) and then in 1922 moved to
164 Queen's Road, where Peckham's only blue plaque
commemorates him. In 1931 Dr Moody was instrumental in
setting up the League of Coloured Peoples, which helped black
people facing discrimination in Britain.

Sir Herman Ouseley, a long-standing Peckham resident who was
born in Guyana, became Chair of the Commission for Racial
Equality and was knighted for his work in 1997. Not far from his
home is a barber's shop at 204 Bellenden Road which was the
focus for a popular TV sitcom called *Desmond's,* starring the West
Indian actor Norman Beaton. It ran for six years on Channel 4
until the final episode was shown in December 1994.

The programme drew on the experiences of West Indian people living in Peckham. They have retained strong links with their families who remained in the Caribbean. Many have worked and saved hard so they could support their relatives and visit them. Second-generation immigrants have absorbed attitudes both from their roots and from local culture. Many have shown considerable talent – for example, West Ham and England footballer Rio Ferdinand who lived in Gisburn House on the Friary Estate for 18 years. He attended Camelot Primary School and spent his leisure time in Leyton Gardens Adventure Playground, Peckham Leisure Centre, North Peckham Library and Peckham Rye Park. He also belonged to a drama club at the Peckham Settlement.

Community organisations have provided opportunities for people from different backgrounds to meet socially and learn from each other. However, many people feel happier and more comfortable with people from their own culture so social gatherings where there are only people of the same background are often held.

Various organisations have been set up to meet the different needs of Peckham's varied population. The African/Caribbean Youth Development Project, Black Elderly Group (Southwark), Caribbean Teachers Association, Karibbean Independent Trust for Ecology, Society of Black Arts, Southwark Asian Centre, Southwark Asian Community Organisation, Southwark Asian Women's Association, Southwark Cypriot Day Centre, Southwark Muslim Women's Association, Southwark Phoenix Women's Health Organisation and Southwark Vietnamese Refugee Association are all based in Peckham.

The population in 1991 of Barset, Bellenden, Consort, Friary, Liddle, The Lane and Waverley wards was 56,566. Within those wards were different percentages of people from ethnic minority backgrounds. In Liddle Ward 56 per cent of the residents were from ethnic minority groups, whereas in The Lane it was only 24 per cent. In Liddle Ward the largest "minority" community was African, forming one-quarter of the population. In The Lane it was the Black Caribbean group which was the largest part of the ethnic population.

Major changes in education

State schools in London were radically reorganised following the Education Act of 1944. The school leaving age was raised from 14 – first to 15, later to 16 – and a division was created between primary schools (up to age 11) and secondary schools for older children.

At age 11 children sat an exam in the final year of primary school – the "11 plus" – and their performance determined their fate. Better-performing children gained places at a grammar school while others were sent to a secondary modern or technical school. The long-term official policy was to introduce "comprehensive" schools, offering education to children of all abilities in a single school. Until this could be achieved, the dual system of grammar schools and secondary moderns was used. There were no grammar schools in Peckham or Nunhead; the nearest were Wilson's (boys), Mary Datchelor (girls) in Camberwell and Aske's in New Cross. Honor Oak School, although an LCC school, was run on grammar lines.

Comprehensives were usually much larger than secondary modern, technical and grammar schools, often having eight forms in each year. They could therefore be introduced only where large enough buildings or sites could be found, and comprehensivisation usually led to the amalgamation of existing schools. The first comprehensives opened in 1948 in outer-London at Hillingdon and Potters Bar.

An extra problem facing education administrators after World War II was finding enough space in schools for the post-war "baby boom". This population bulge peaked in primary schools in the mid-1950s and in secondary schools in the early-1960s.

The body dealing with these difficulties was the London County Council, which ran most schools until 1965, when the Inner London Education Authority (ILEA) took over following the abolition of the LCC and creation of the Greater London Council. ILEA was abolished in 1990 and Southwark Council then became responsible for running most schools in Peckham and Nunhead.

There was no difficulty in coping with the baby boom in Peckham's primary schools – there were ten large primary

schools in the early post-war period. Subsequently a number of
them were renamed, for example Bird in Bush School was
rechristened Camelot, Ruby Street School was called Watling
and Wood's Road became John Donne. An example of new
provision at primary level was the creation of Pilgrim's Way
Primary School in Manor Grove which was officially opened
on 21 March 1969 by Sir Louis Gluckstein, Chairman of the
Greater London Council. The school was built to serve the
new Tustin Estate.

In 1948 there were seven secondary schools in Peckham:
Colls Road, Honor Oak, Leo Street near Asylum Road, Peckham
in Choumert Road and Peckham Road, Adys Road and Peckham
Rye in Whorlton Road. A number of these amalgamated to
form larger comprehensives. For example in the early 1950s
Peckham Central School in Choumert Road joined with Adys
Road to form William Penn School. William Penn moved to Red
Post Hill in 1958. Thomas Calton, previously in East Dulwich,
then occupied these buildings. Waverley School was created in
1978 by merging Honor Oak School in Homestall Road with
Friern Lower School. Five years later, in September 1983,
Warwick Park School was established by the amalgamation
of Peckham School, Peckham Manor, Silverthorne in
Southampton Way and Thomas Calton.

With the passing of the baby boom some Peckham secondary
schools closed: for example Collingwood School in York Grove,
which in 1982 amalgamated with Samuel Pepys School to become
Hatcham Wood School.

The LCC also provided special schools such as Bredinghurst
School, Stuart Road, opened in 1948 in a building erected in 1874
and previously used by the Camberwell Poor Law Union as a
children's home. Bredinghurst School was the first school for
maladjusted children in the country to incorporate in its structure
a full psychiatric unit. A new building for Elfrida Rathbone
School was opened in 1965; the school's name was changed to
Haymerle School in 1992. Highshore School, in Bellenden Road,

was opened in 1970 to replace a building erected on the same site in 1889. Tuke School, built on the site of St Mark's Church in Harder's (now Woods) Road, was also opened in 1970.

Operating in parallel with the LCC or county schools were voluntary-aided schools funded partly by the LCC and partly by religious denominations. There was one secondary school of this type: St Thomas the Apostle Roman Catholic School (now College) which opened in 1965 in Hollydale Road on a site where a private school run by the Marist Sisters once stood.

Roman Catholic primary schools include St Francis School in Friary Road and St James the Great (until 1996, St Alban's). St James occupies the building once used by the County Secondary School on Peckham Road. St John's and St Clement's, a Church of England primary school, also occupies a recycled building: it moved in 1994 from Northcross Road into what was once the Adys Road School.

The Ann Bernadt Nursery and Early Learning Centre, in Chandler Way, was opened by Harriet Harman, MP in 1997. It commemorates Ann Bernadt (1948-96) who was elected to the Inner London Education Authority for Dulwich in 1986 and to Southwark Council in 1990.

Apart from changes in buildings and administration, education today is considerably different from in the immediate post-war period. Schools have taken advantage of modern technology to enable pupils to become computer-literate from an early age. Subjects are no longer taught in rigid compartments and there is far more experiential learning. The curriculum is more geared to the world of work and pupils have work experience before they leave school. There is also less emphasis on examinations and more on continuous assessment.

After leaving school, young people in Peckham and Nunhead have more opportunities for continuing their learning and development through Southwark College and other educational establishments.

Commercial eras end

Rye Lane was noted as one of South London's major shopping centres and was known as the "Golden Mile". Its decline began in 1949 when Holdron's large store closed. Part of the firm's chimney can be seen in the Copeland Industrial Park.

From the 1970s Rye Lane found it increasingly difficult to cope with competition from shopping centres at Lewisham, Bromley and Croydon. A major blow hit Rye Lane when Jones and Higgins closed on 7 June 1980 after over a century as Peckham's leading store. It reopened two days later as The Houndsditch in Peckham but the store, apart from the section containing the clock tower, was demolished in 1985. The Aylesham Centre, named after a Kent mining village, was built on the site. In the 1980s and 1990s Rye Lane saw the closure of well-known stores including the Royal Arsenal Co-operative Society, British Home Stores, C&A, Dunn & Co and Marks & Spencer.

Sainsbury's last old-style shop, where assistants served behind different counters, was at 61-63 Rye Lane until 1982. It was replaced by a supermarket which had a short life (1982-93); this was converted into the Premier Cinema. Tesco's also closed their small store in Rye Lane.

Increasingly in the 1980s and 1990s, shops in Rye Lane were run by and for people whose roots lay in various countries around the world, including the West Indies, West Africa, Turkey and Vietnam. As a result, produce that was not available in Peckham before World War II is now widely available – for example, yams, breadfruit, green bananas and mangoes. Choumert Road Market, which has existed since the late 1870s, now specialises in Afro-Caribbean foods.

At Peckham Rye an era ended when Austin's closed on 5 November 1994. Derek and Valerie Austin were unable to find anyone to buy their old and highly regarded firm, one of the largest second-hand and antique dealers in Europe. Austins Court now occupies the site. Another era ended in Nunhead in 1981 when the Gandolfi brothers ceased production of wooden hand-made cameras. The centenary of the Gandolfi enterprise had been marked by a special

Holdron's in Rye Lane. A view of c.1927.

exhibition at the Science Museum only the year before. Inner
London's last cowkeeper was John Jorden who ran a dairy with
30-40 cows in Lugard Road until 1967.

Samuel Jones' gummed paper factory in Peckham Grove was
demolished in 1982; the Samuel Jones Industrial Estate was built
on the site. The closure of the Peckham branch of the Grand
Surrey Canal caused Abbey Rose builders' merchants to leave
Canal Head in 1988; they took the opportunity to move to larger
premises in Blackpool Road.

Growth in car ownership resulted in the Old Kent Road becoming
a venue for large retail warehouses. The Cantium Retail Park, at
the junction with Olmar Street, was opened in 1992 and sells
electrical goods, DIY products and hamburgers to customers from
a large area of south-east London.

During the last 20 years there has been a growth in stores that
are part of large chains and a fall in the number of independent
shops. Food superstores have caused the closure of shops run by
independent grocers, butchers, greengrocers and bakers. Rye
Lane has changed considerably but maintains a variety of shops
that cater for the needs of local people.

Public services develop

The Pioneer Health Centre resumed its activities in 1946. During World War II its building in St Mary's Road had remained empty until 1942 and had then been rented as a factory by makers of radar equipment for four years. Shortly after the Centre's post-war reopening, the Foreign Office proposed that a film *The Centre* should be made for distribution in foreign countries. The first public showing took place at the Odeon in Peckham High Street in July 1948. Her Majesty Queen Mary saw the film and then went to the Centre, which she had first visited in 1939. The Prime Minister, Clement Attlee, and many other distinguished guests were also present. The film was subsequently shown all over the world in eight different languages. Sadly, the Centre ran out of money and closed in 1950.

The National Health Service, which started two years before the Centre closed, aimed to improve people's health but refused to fund the Centre. General practitioners worked single-handed in the 1940s. In 1953 there was only one group practice but a few decades later these became the norm. New centres were built, such as the Isidore Crown Medical Centre in Chadwick Road, which was opened in 1998 by Tessa Jowell, MP for Dulwich and West Norwood and Britain's first Minister of State for Public Health. This modern Medical Centre replaced the terraced house at 105 Bellenden Road in which Dr Crown started in 1953.

When the Camden Estate was built in the 1970s, the Lister Health Centre, named after Lord Lister, was included in the estate – as was the Helena Day Nursery which commemorated Councillor Helena Day.

Peckham Pulse, Britain's first healthy living centre, opened on 6 June 1998 adjacent to Peckham Square. It was called Pulse because of connotations with health and fitness. Among its facilities are a swimming pool, health and fitness suite, hydrotherapy pool, children's soft play area, creche, massage, relaxation and fitness classes and a cafe with a view across the linear park. When Peckham Pulse was planned, some information and inspiration were gleaned from the Pioneer Health Centre.

Peckham Police Station was rebuilt and opened by Her Royal
Highness Princess Alexandra on 10 March 1988. A new Peckham
Fire Station was opened in Peckham Road on 2 March 1991.

A prefabricated library was opened in Peckham Hill Street in
1954. This replaced Camberwell Central Library, which had been
bombed, and stood where Kingfisher House is today. A new
library, with a dramatic design by architects Alsop & Störmer, is
due to open in 1999 and will include South London's first African
and Caribbean Literature Centre.

North Peckham Civic Centre and Library opened in 1966,
adjacent to Canal Bridge which was demolished in 1992-93.
The two outside walls are decorated with a striking tiled ceramic
frieze by the Polish sculptor Adam Kossowski depicting episodes
in the history of the Old Kent Road. A short distance away is the
Livesey Museum opened by Sir John Betjeman in 1974. This
building originally housed the first public library in Camberwell;
it was the gift of George Livesey, whose statue was moved to the
Museum's courtyard from the gasworks across the road.

In 1979 there was a controversial proposal to build a huge civic
centre to accommodate all council headquarters' staff on a site at
the junction of Rye Lane and Peckham High Street. The proposal
received outline planning permission but proceeded no further.

New parks and green spaces

In 1943 the London County Council produced a plan for the
future of London. It recommended that there should be seven
acres of open space per thousand people. In accordance with the
Town and Country Planning Act 1947, the LCC published the
Initial Development Plan in 1951. It included proposals for the
creation of North Camberwell Open Space, which developed into
Burgess Park. It was named after Jessie Burgess who was
Camberwell's first woman Mayor (1945–47) and was a councillor
for 44 years.

The park was developed in piecemeal fashion. The work of creating the park was started by the LCC and continued first by the Greater London Council and then by Southwark Council. Today Groundwork Southwark is spearheading the development programme for a park that is unique in Britain as it was created in an inner city area by demolishing houses and industrial buildings. The linear park from Peckham Square follows the line of the Grand Surrey Canal to Burgess Park. The impressive arch, with its unusual lighting that changes with the atmosphere, was added in 1994.

When the disused lake on Peckham Rye was filled in during 1953, an additional grassed area was provided on the northern part of the common.

The importance of green spaces was recognised by town planners and councillors. Warwick Gardens, named after Alderman Alfred Charles Warwick who was Mayor of Camberwell 1935-36, was opened in 1963. Cossall Park was created, where Victorian houses had stood, when the Cossall Estate was built in the 1970s. Brimmington Park, Consort Park, Bird in Bush Park and Highshore Shrubbery were also provided so that residents could have a small park close to their homes. These new parks were much simpler and cheaper to maintain than ornate Victorian ones.

Rosemary Gardens, which was created in 1960, was built on during the 1990s as part of a home-building project under the Peckham Partnership Scheme. Three small parks in North Peckham will replace the three acres that were lost.

The London Wildlife Trust opened a Wildlife Garden Centre in a disused Southwark Council yard in Marsden Road in 1989. This was done because of the need to grow hundreds of trees to replace those lost in Peckham and other parts of London during the Great Storm of 16 October 1987. Since then this community-led project has specialised in encouraging wildlife gardening. The London Wildlife Trust also created nature gardens in McDermott Road, Goldsmith Road and Bellenden Road. In addition, the Trust assisted Southwark Council in digging up an unused part of Kirkwood Road and converting it into a nature reserve.

The residents of Choumert Square, which was built between 1876 and 1882, grew so many flowers and shrubs that it was described by *The Guardian* as "a blooming alley in Peckham". Nearby the Sri Chinmoy Peace Garden was built on derelict land in the grounds of the Thomas Calton Education Centre in Alpha Street. It was opened on 15 July 1991 by Sri Chinmoy, an Indian philosopher and musician whose work aims to promote peace between communities and nations.

Nunhead Cemetery became increasingly neglected by its owners, the London Cemetery Company. In the early 1970s there was talk of closing the cemetery and selling the site for redevelopment, but an action group was formed to try to protect the interests of people who had owned burial rights or who had relatives interred at Nunhead. Largely as a result of the action group's efforts, Southwark Council stepped in to purchase the cemetery for £1 in 1975. Six years later, the Friends of Nunhead Cemetery was formed to promote and care for the cemetery as a place of historical and ecological interest and beauty as well as a burial ground. The cemetery has a large number of mature trees and its atmosphere is enhanced by the many subsiding tombstones. Southwark Council and the Friends are working together to improve the cemetery, which has attracted lottery money for restoration and to create a visitor centre in one of the Victorian lodges.

New places of worship

World War II was very destructive to Peckham's churches. Most church buildings were damaged or destroyed.

Two Anglican churches had to be totally rebuilt after the war – St Luke's, in Pentridge Street, and St Mary Magdalene in St Mary's Road. St John's was built on the site of St Jude's in Meeting House Lane. St Antholin's, Nunhead Lane, was rebuilt and renamed St Antony's. The spire of Christ Church in the Old Kent Road was removed when the church was restored.

Some other bombed churches were not rebuilt after the war. These
included St Mark's, where Tuke School is today in Woods Road;
Avondale Road Unitarian Church, where 15 and 17 Avondale Rise
are today; and the Dissenters' chapel in Nunhead Cemetery.

As the 20th century wore on, old church buildings were replaced
with new ones "to serve the present age" and reflecting the
decline in attendance since the original churches were built.
These included Peckham Methodist, St George's and Peckham
Rye Tabernacle. St Saviour's was converted into a church-cum-
community centre; it was renamed The Copleston Centre.

All Saints' in Davey Street had an unusual afterlife following its
demolition. All the bricks, stone and wood were transported to
Biggin Hill, where the materials were used to build a new church.
The remarkable story is told in *The Moving Church* by Vivian
Symons, the vicar responsible for the enterprise. A pictorial
display of the way the church was moved from Peckham can be
seen inside St Mark's, Biggin Hill.

The growth in the West Indian and West African population
resulted in an increasing demand for church buildings in the
1980s and 1990s. Some redundant churches, which had been
taken over by commercial firms, were brought back into use as
churches – such as the former Corpus Christi College Cambridge
Mission, Waverley Park Methodist Church and Nunhead Baptist
Church Congregations without buildings increasingly hired other
churches when they were not being used by the denomination
that owned them. In addition, commercial buildings were taken
over for use as churches. These included the former C&A
premises in Rye Lane (South London Temple), 176 Rye Lane
(Universal Church of the Kingdom of God) and 133 Copeland
Industrial Park (Holy Emmanuel Church of Christ).

The different ethnic traditions of the population were reflected
in church buildings that changed denominations. Hanover Chapel
(United Reformed Church) in Bellenden Road became Faith Chapel
when it was bought by a Pentecostal congregation. St Andrew's in
Glengall Road was taken over by the Celestial Church of Christ, a
Nigerian church. Apostolic Faith Church took over a London City

Mission hall in Fenham Road. By the 1990s SE15 had more black
Pentecostal churches than any other denomination.

Other churches were demolished during the post-war period
including Clifton Congregational, where Clifton Court is in
Asylum Road today, Peckham Rye Congregational in Linden
Grove and St Chrysostom's in Peckham Hill Street.

People with faiths other than Christian acquired their own places
of worship such as the Peckham Islamic Centre in Choumert
Grove, which had been a school building, and the New Peckham
Mosque which uses the former St Mark's Church in Cobourg Road.

Leisure: a wide choice

The post-war period saw a great increase in the range of leisure
activities available to the people of Peckham. Cinemas remained
popular after World War II, but attendances gradually declined
as ownership of televisions increased and homes became more
comfortable. The Tower Cinema closed in 1956 and the site
became a car park. The entrance has recently been renovated and
will include a zoetrope, an optical device from the early days of
the 20th century in which a viewer looks through a slit in the
side of a cylinder at pictures engraved on the inside – and as the
cylinder spins the pictures appear to move.

The Astoria in the Old Kent Road closed in 1968 but was not
demolished until 1984. The site is now occupied by a store
belonging to the home improvements firm Magnet. After the Ace
Cinema, previously called the Odeon, closed in 1983, Peckham
had no cinema until the Premier opened in 1994. Like many
modern cinemas, the Premier is a multiscreen.

Cinemas that closed after World War II were often converted
into bingo halls, as this gambling craze grew. The Gaumont in
Peckham High Street became the first Top Rank Bingo Club
in 1961 but the club closed in November 1998 as a result of
falling attendances.

Public houses declined in popularity, partly because more people drank wine and canned beers at home. Some pubs therefore closed and were converted for other uses. The Surrey View Tavern became a cafe, the Golddiggers Arms was made into offices and the Sailor Prince is now flats. Other pubs kept going by offering a wider range of entertainments – for example, large-screen television broadcasts of sporting events.

The lido on Peckham Rye – which was featured in the 1969 film *Entertaining Mr Sloane* – was closed in April 1987. A circus and fair usually visit the Rye each year.

Southwark Council opened the Peckham Leisure Centre in McKerrell Road in 1986. It included a sports hall the size of four badminton courts, a fitness room, changing rooms, a bar and a creche. Table tennis, netball, hockey, trampolining and football were some of the sports available. Gymnastics, keep-fit, indoor bowls, dance classes and indoor athletics were also all on offer. Peckham Pulse, included on page 84, is an exciting addition to leisure facilities in Peckham.

A bright future beckons

Under the Local Government Act 1963, 32 London boroughs were created and the Greater London Council superseded the London County Council. The Metropolitan Boroughs of Bermondsey, Camberwell and Southwark were amalgamated to form the London Borough of Southwark in 1965. Since then, councillors and council staff have worked hard to improve Peckham and Nunhead in co-operation with local residents.

A wide variety of people and organisations are working together to ensure that the quality of life in Peckham and Nunhead continues to improve. Led by Southwark Council, the Peckham Partnership started to implement one of the country's largest regeneration programmes in April 1995. The aim of the Partnership is to make Peckham "a place where people choose to live, work and visit".

Among the organisations and people who are partners in this major enterprise are: the Housing Corporation; housing associations; private building firms; forums involving local people; schools; traders; the Metropolitan Police; the Inner London Probation Service; the Lambeth, Southwark and Lewisham Health Authority; bus and railway firms; London University Institute of Education; and the Government Office for London.

By the year 2002 the Peckham Partnership aims to have demolished more than 3,000 properties and built more than 2,000 new homes; reduced unemployment by creating hundreds of jobs; helped more than 800 people to achieve recognised qualifications; increased the number of people shopping in Peckham town centre; increased educational attainment at local schools; trained young people in sports and leisure; provided a new library, media, education and training facility; reduced crime; built a new health and fitness centre and improved the health of local residents.

Groundwork Southwark is spearheading improvements to the post-war Burgess Park. Friends of Peckham Rye Park and Southwark Council are co-operating to refurbish the Victorian park adjacent to Peckham Rye common. The Friends of Nunhead Cemetery are working with the council to improve the cemetery and to provide facilities for visitors.

Peckham Pulse, 1998.

Grove Vale Renewal Forum, assisted by Southwark Community Planning and Education Centre, has produced imaginative plans for the site of the Grove Vale Depot to be redeveloped for the benefit of residents in East Dulwich and South Peckham. The depot is in the Bellenden Renewal Area, where housing and the environment are being improved in a special programme.

All developments in SE15 are closely monitored by The Peckham Society, which exists to encourage interest in the environment and history of the area and to care for it. The Peckham Society has proposed that a piazza be created in front of the entrance to Peckham Rye Station. It is also keeping a close eye on any plans for the Peckham Rye Lido site to ensure that appropriate use be made of the common land on which the lido was built. The Peckham Society is also keen for the central part of the former steam bus garage in Nunhead Lane to be preserved, as the building is unique in London if not in the whole of the UK.

Southwark Council has redevelopment plans to improve shopping on the north side of Peckham High Street. An attempt to bring the London Underground to Peckham in the first decade of the 20th century failed, but the East London line may yet be extended to Queen's Road, Peckham Rye and East Dulwich stations in the 21st century. The Bakerloo Line may also have new stations at Camberwell and Peckham.

At the end of the 20th century Peckham is going through a period of remarkable change – but this is certainly not a new experience for the area. Peckham and Nunhead have evolved over many centuries and have been left with a rich heritage in their numerous interesting styles of architecture and countless surviving records that tell us about people who lived in the area. This wealth continues in the district's current rich ethnic diversity, which provides so much of Peckham and Nunhead's vibrancy and character.

Southwark Council, a multitude of organisations and all the people who live in SE15 have a vital role to play in helping the area to develop in positive ways. As the district continues to improve, residents should feel increasingly proud to live in Peckham and Nunhead.

Booklist

Allport, Douglas, *Camberwell and Neighbourhood* (1841)

Batten, Rex, *The Leysdown Tragedy* (Friends of Nunhead Cemetery, 1992)

Batten, Rex, *Nunhead Remembered* (Friends of Nunhead Cemetery, 1995)

Beasley, John D., *Who Was Who in Peckham* (Chener Books, 1985)

Beasley, John D., *Building Together* (Peckham Methodist Church, 1985)

Beasley, John D., *Origin of Names in Peckham and Nunhead* (South Riding Press, 1993)

Beasley, John D., *Peckham and Nunhead Churches* (South Riding Press, 1995)

Beasley, John D., *Peckham Rye Park Centenary* (South Riding Press, 1995)

Beasley, John D., *Peckham and Nunhead: The Archive Photographs Series* (Tempus Publishing, 1995)

Beasley, John D., *Transport in Peckham and Nunhead* (South Riding Press, 1997)

Beasley, John D., *East Dulwich* (South Riding Press, 1998)

Blanch, W.H., *Ye Parish of Camerwell* (E.W. Allen, 1875) Facsmile reprint published by Stephen Marks for The Camberwell Society (1976)

Besant, Sir Walter, *London South of the Thames* (Adam & Charles Black, 1912)

Charlesworth, Tim, *The Architecture of Peckham* (Chener Books, 1988)

Cherry, Bridget, and Pevsner, Nikolaus, *The Buildings of England LONDON 2: SOUTH* (Penguin, 1983)

Crown, Isidore, *Take One Acecdote Twice Daily* (Book Guild, 1993)

Crown, Isidore, *Repeat Prescription* (Keter Classics, 1996)

Crown, Isidore, *No Side Effects* (Keter Classics, 1998)

Curl, James Stevens, *Nunhead Cemetery, London* (Ancient Monuments Society, 1977)

Dyos, H.J., *Victorian Suburb* (Leicester University Press, 1996)

Edwards, J., *Companion from London to Brighthelmston* (1801)

Goss, Sue, *Local Labour and Local Government* (Edinburgh University Press, 1988)

Harley, Robert J., *Camberwell & West Norwood Tramways including Dulwich and Peckham* (Middleton Press, 1993)

Harris, Stephen, *Old Surviving Firms of South London* (The author, 1987)

Humphrey, Stephen, *Britain in Old Photographs: Camberwell, Dulwich and Peckham* (Sutton, 1996)

King, Sam, *Climbing up the rough side of the mountain* (Minerva Press, 1998)

Manning, Owen, and Bray, William, *The history and antiquities of the County of Surrey* (John White, 1804)

Marcan, Peter, *Visions of Southwark* (Peter Marcan Publications, 1997)

Marshall, W.W., *The Peckham Partnership Development Handbook* (Southwark Challenge Partnership Management Board, 1994)

Mee, Arthur, *The King's England: LONDON* (Hodder and Stoughton, 1937)

Mitchell, Vic, and Smith, Keith, *South London Line* (Middleton Press, 1995)

Nisbet, John, *The Story of the One Tree Hill Agitation, with a short sketch of the history of Honor Oak Hill* (Centenary Edition reprinted 1997, Michael Counsell)

Nunhead Cemetery: An Illustrated Guide (Friends of Nunhead Cemetery, 1988)

Pearse, Innes H., *The Quality of Life* (Scottish Academic Press, 1979)

Pearse, Innes H. and Crocker, Lucy H., *The Peckham Experiment* (Scottish Academic Press, 1985)

Peckham and Camberwell Illustrated (1892)

Potter, George, *Father Potter of Peckham* (Hodder and Stoughton, 1955)

Potter, George, *More Father Potter of Peckham* (Hodder and Stoughton, 1958)

Reilly, Leonard, *Southwark: An Illustrated History* (London Borough of Southwark, 1998)

Spark, Muriel, *The Ballad of Peckham Rye* (Macmillan, 1960)

Stallibrass, Alison, *Being Me and Also Us: Lessons from the Peckham Experiment* (Scottish Academic Press, 1989)

Steele, Jess (Ed), *The Streets of London: The Booth Notebooks - South East* (Deptford Forum Publishing, 1997)

Tames, Richard, *Dulwich and Camberwell Past with Peckham* (Historical Publications, 1997)

Thomas, John Birch, *Shop Boy: An Autobiography* (Routledge & Kegan Paul, 1983)

Tilling, John, *Kings of the Highway* (Hutchinson, 1957)

Vaughan, David A., *Negro Victory: The life story of Dr Harold Moody* (Independent Press, 1950)

Victoria History of the Counties of England - Surrey (University of London Institute of Historical Research, 1967)

Walford, Edward, *Old and New London* (Cassell Peter Galpin, n.d.)

Williamson, G. Scott, and Pearse, I.H., *Biologists in search of material* (Faber & Faber, 1938)

Woollacott, Ron, *A Historical Tour of Nunhead and Peckham Rye* (Maureen and Ron Woollacott, 1995)

Woollacott, Ron, *Nunhead Notables* (Friends of Nunhead Cemetery, 1984)

Woollacott, Ron, *More Nunhead Notables* (Friends of Nunhead Cemetery, 1995)

Maps
Old Ordnance Survey Maps published by Alan Godfrey: Brockley 1868; Deptford (North) 1914; East Dulwich & Peckham Rye 1868 and 1914; New Cross 1914; Old Kent Road 1894 and 1914; Peckham 1914.

Index